Focus Group Research

Qualitative Essentials

Series Editor: Janice Morse
University of Utah

Series Editorial Board: H. Russell Bernard, Kathy Charmaz, D. Jean Clandinin, Juliet Corbin, Carmen de la Cuesta, John Engel, Sue E. Estroff, Jane Gilgun, Jeffrey C. Johnson, Carl Mitcham, Katja Mruck, Judith Preissle, Jean J. Schensul, Sally Thorne, John van Maanen, Max van Manen

Qualitative Essentials is a book series providing a comprehensive but succinct overview of topics in qualitative inquiry. These books will fill an important niche in qualitative methods for students—and others new to the qualitative research—who require rapid but complete perspective on specific methods, strategies, and important topics. Written by leaders in qualitative inquiry, alone or in combination, these books will be an excellent resource for instructors and students from all disciplines. Proposals for the series should be sent to the series editor at explore@lcoastpress.com.

Titles in this series:

Focus Group Research

Martha Ann Carey

Jo-Ellen Asbury

Walnut Creek, California

LEFT COAST PRESS, INC.
1630 North Main Street, #400
Walnut Creek, CA 94596
www.LCoastPress.com

ISBN 978-1-61132-255-2 hardcover
ISBN 978-1-61132-256-9 paperback
ISBN 978-1-61132-694-9 consumer eBook

Library of Congress Cataloging-in-Publication Data:

Carey, Martha Ann, 1939-
Focus group research / Martha Ann Carey, Jo-Ellen Asbury.
     p. cm. — (Qualitative essentials; 9)
     Includes bibliographical references and index.
     ISBN 978-1-61132-255-2 (hardback : alk. paper) — ISBN 978-1-61132-256-9 (pbk. : alk. paper) — ISBN 978-1-61132-694-9 (consumer eBook)
     1. Focus groups. 2. Social sciences—Research—Methodology. I. Asbury, Jo-Ellen. II. Title.
H61.28.C37 2012
001.4'33—dc23
                              2012021421

Printed in the United States of America

⊛™ The paper used in this publication meets the minimum requirements of American National Standard for Information Sciences—Permanence of Paper for Printed Library Materials, ANSI/NISO Z39.48–1992.

Contents

To the Azusa Pacific University doctoral nursing students, who helped me to realize anew the excitement of learning to find the "hidden meanings"; to the late Mickey J. W. Smith, who was my colleague as we both were learning; to Margaret Juliano for patience and many hours of research support; and to Mary Thompson, who helped me persevere.

—Martha Ann Carey

To the memory of my mother, Wilhelmina Jefferson Asbury (1918–2008), who taught me many valuable lessons, including how to move through an imperfect world with dignity and grace. And to my daughter, Amanda Asbury Young, who is my inspiration, daily, to honor my mother's teachings. And to the rest of the Asbury clan: thank you for simply being there.

—Jo-Ellen Asbury

Foreword

Martin Tolich

Merton and colleagues (Merton, Kendal, and Fiske, 1990) may have developed focus groups as a bona fide research technique, but it is understanding the psychosocial "group effect" that provides the explanation for how focus groups work so well to elicit sound information from semistructured, informal groups. *"A group session has chemistry and dynamic that are more than the sum of its members' comments."* Carey and Asbury's concise book, *Focus Group Research*, draws on decades of their research using focus groups in a vast array of settings.

Focus Group Research delves into the dynamics of focus groups: how informants could censor themselves, how group members might conform to the group expectations, and how synergies between members unwittingly transform the flow of conversation. Together these group dynamics paradoxically realize both the strength of focus groups and their potential weakness. *"The apparent ease of use can lead researchers to underestimate the challenges and pitfalls."* Carey and Asbury's chapter on analyzing focus group data is unique in the literature and particularly helpful. This chapter not only reviews a range of theoretical perspectives—thematic analysis, discourse analysis, content analysis, narrative analysis, and grounded theory—but also gives a sound basis for understanding data within the group setting.

Focus Group Research is the first handbook to provide a critical reflective account of focus group ethics at all stages of the research. Central to this reflectivity is how Carey and Asbury isolate the ethics staple confidentiality as potentially problematic for focus group researchers: confidentiality is not a given in focus group research. Whereas a researcher may promise to keep all informants' information confidential, the researcher cannot assure confidentiality. That is, the researcher cannot guarantee the research participants that other focus group members will not make public the statements others made inside the focus group session. In addition, participants may disclose more than they intended. This ethical reflectivity represents a coming of age for this previously considered innocuous data-collection technique.

Although vulnerable groups (children, the elderly, LGBT [lesbian, gay, bisexual, transgender], those with cognitive disability) have traditionally been viewed as not appropriate participants for focus groups, Carey and Asbury target these groups as appropriate participants. Focus groups reduce power imbalances between researcher and participant, thereby empowering them and facilitating research with them rather than on them. Carey and Asbury give specific and valuable advice on how to maximize results from vulnerable groups. For the elderly, logistical planning should involve access to the focus group, physical comfort, and auditory acuity. For children, issues include optimal group size, the duration of the session, and how gender differences function at different ages. Chapter 7 provides one of the few descriptions of how to communicate focus group research findings.

Focus Group Research is essential reading for postgraduates in health, the social sciences, and education. The size of the book belies how much information is packed between its covers. It is a quick how-to read, yet the reader will want to spend considerable time to digest the vast array of information provided. Guides to further reading are included within each chapter. The book gives novice researchers and experienced qualitative researchers using focus groups for the first time sound guidance on how to utilize focus groups effectively.

Preface

Much of qualitative research involves looking deep for meaning that is not immediately apparent. As we worked on this book, we were reminded of the long ago practice of hiding messages in quilt designs as a means of providing directions to slaves trying to escape from slavery in the South via the underground railroad—a covert way of travel to freedom in the North. The slave owners saw the quilts as an everyday sight, without recognizing the invisible codes that the slaves learned to read (Tobin and Dobard, 1999). We believe that focus groups are analogous to those historic quilts; such groups are an effective method of looking deeper when conducting social science research.

Focus groups have been used very widely—from market research to rigorous social science research. The apparent ease of using focus groups can lead some to underestimate the challenges and pitfalls. This book provides the knowledge needed to plan and implement rigorous, high-quality data collection, analyze that data, interpret the findings, and report the results of the group studies for optimal validity and usefulness.

The intended audience for this book is researchers who have some familiarity with qualitative research methods but may be new to focus group research. This text would also be useful to graduate students taking a course in qualitative methods. Topics include a brief description of the background and history of focus groups, the conceptual framework that informs this method, the basic elements for developing a research plan, guidance for planning and conducting sessions, considerations for special populations, and recommendations for data analysis and reporting findings. Attention to ethics and rigor is essential throughout research, and these concerns are addressed throughout the book. Each chapter begins with questions to alert you to key concepts.

Our objective for this book is provide the insight necessary for you to think through and plan your study in ways that improve your research question, data collection and analysis, and credibility of findings. The usefulness of your study will be improved by understanding the logical links between the conceptual framework (sociology, psychology, and psychosocial concepts) and good qualitative research design.

Acknowledgments

Several people helped make this book possible, too many to list individually. We are particularly grateful to Jan Morse for her inspiration and encouragement, to Lois-ellin Datta for helpful comments on an early draft, and to Stevenson University for supporting Jo-Ellen's work on this project and for access to library resources.

Martha Ann Carey
Jo-Ellen Asbury
June 2012

1. What Is a Focus Group?

This chapter presents the basics of the focus group technique as a research method used in social science studies. Topics include the definition of *focus group* and a brief history, advantages of this approach, information about when not to use this method, recent developments involving computer technology, rigor, ethics, and common criticisms.

Key Questions

1.1. When and why would you use a focus group?

1.2. How would you address common criticisms, such as unwieldy sessions and the collection of only minimal information?

Definition

The purpose of using focus groups is to collect rich, detailed data. Descriptions of a focus group vary but usually include a semistructured session, an informal setting, moderation by a facilitator and possibly a cofacilitator, and the use of general guideline questions and/or other stimuli, such as photos (Krueger and Casey, 2009; Morgan, 2010; Stewart, Shadasani, and Rook, 2009). Although consensus development, emotional support, and/or education may be part of a focus group session, these are generally not the purpose of a study that uses focus groups to collect data. Although in understanding the data one must take into account the context, a study of group process per se is not considered the goal of a focus group study. Data collection is focused on the topic selected, not on the process of the group interaction.

Focus Group Research by Martha-Ann Carey and Jo-Ellen Asbury, 15–26 © 2012 Left Coast Press, Inc. All rights reserved.

Focus groups generally consist of a one-time meeting of persons who do not know one another and who have a common experience, such as the death of a child or experience as a caregiver for an elderly parent. But it is becoming more common to use focus groups in settings where the members do know one another and expect to have continued contact. This situation presents some challenges for the quality of the data and is discussed in a later section.

Published articles using focus groups have become so popular that the term *focus group* is not generally used as a "keyword" in literature searches. Although this term is broadly used, and sometimes misused, this book focuses on social science studies.

What makes focus groups so popular? They are intuitively appealing. People like to be heard; they want to feel that someone is listening and understanding their concerns. Researchers with some "people skills" like to engage participants, especially persons from communities who often do not have a voice in matters that affect them. When sessions have been arranged so that participants feel comfortable and the facilitator is well prepared, the conversation is usually very engaging and leads to rich stories that likely would not be told in such detail in another type of study. We have often been surprised in our focus groups at the level of detail and the candidness of the experiences described.

The development of the focus group approach is mostly associated with the research programs of Paul Lazarsfeld, Robert Merton, and colleagues (Merton, Fiske, and Kendall, 1990). Although group interviews had been used before World War II, little attention was given to this approach until studies were done of the effectiveness of radio programs during the war in the 1940s (Morgan, 1993). Since then, marketing studies have extensively used this approach, and in the last twenty or so years politicians have been using data collected through focus groups to help shape their campaigns. In addition, the social sciences have increasingly used this approach in the fields of education, nursing, psychology, social work, and sociology.

Focus groups are best suited to environments and groups in which the members are knowledgeable, willing, and capable of communicating; the topic and the group setting are compatible to group interaction; and the group facilitator has adequate skills. Persons are able to participate when they share a common language and an important experience. Accommodations can be made to enhance the ability of the members in the group to participate, such as providing hearing-assistance devices for the hearing-impaired and arranging shorter sessions for certain elderly or ill people who may not be able to sit for long periods of time. In determining whether a focus group is an appropriate research method, keep in mind that the focus group is the method, a tool for achieving the task. As Heidegger stated, "it is not the hammer that the carpenter focuses on, but the nail and the table" (in Kvale, 1996, p. 107). In this analogy, the focus group approach is the hammer, and the research data involve the nail and the table.

Focus groups are planned to capitalize on the interaction among the group members to enhance the collection of deep, strongly held beliefs and perspectives. This approach, like most qualitative methods, is especially useful for exploring new topics and examining complex issues. Behavior and beliefs can be especially useful in situations in which there is little information to serve as a foundation for your research, when no instruments exist to study the question at hand, or when an explanation of the processes behind the action is needed. With appropriate guidance from the group facilitator, the group setting can enhance candor and spontaneity.

As with other qualitative methods, focus groups can be used in an integrated design (mixed methods) with quantitative data and also with data obtained with other qualitative methods. Each type of data can be integrated to inform various aspects of the overall research question. These issues are discussed in a later chapter.

The focus group technique is not primarily a consensus-building technique. For some purposes, it could be used to obtain agreement, but that could limit the richness and breadth of experiences shared. However, some members may understand the group's role to be consensus, and therefore they may believe that each guideline question needs to be resolved by mutual agreement. The group facilitator has the responsibility to help members to understand what is expected of them. Although people do use the opinions of others in forming their own opinions, the tendency toward consensus is particularly a problem when a member's opinion is not yet formed and therefore his or her participation or contributions could be affected by comments made in the group session. This effect, sometimes referred to as the bandwagon effect, lessens the meaningfulness of the data.

Advantages

Focus groups can provide insights into attitudes and beliefs that underlie behavior and by providing context and perspective that enable experiences to be understood more holistically. Members' descriptions of experiences can provide unique information on how members give meaning to and organize their experiences.

Focus groups can "give voice" to members of vulnerable populations who might not be heard as well with other approaches. For many studies, this method allows for complex issues to be explored with richer data than individual interviews would elicit. The synergy in the group interaction usually prompts greater breadth and depth of information, and comparison of views within a group leads to greater insight into experiences.

In community-based participatory research, focus groups are especially useful when the method of discussion is a natural fit with the local culture. Studying the concept of wellness from the perspective of elderly Native Hawaiians, Odell (2008) successfully used focus groups on the island of Hawai'i. The focus group discussions were very similar to the Hawaiian custom of "talk story," which is talking for long periods of time about daily life and concerns. The comfort of the members with the focus group technique certainly added to the rich, new data that were collected.

Situations Not Appropriate for Focus Groups

Focus groups are not always the most appropriate methodological choice. Similar to other qualitative techniques, focus groups are not the method of choice when the research question involves the magnitude of a problem, including how many individuals or how large a population is involved with a particular issue. In some instances, a taboo subject may be better captured in an individual interview or via a computer than in a group setting. However, there is some evidence that groups may facilitate the discussion of sensitive topics (Kitzinger, 1994; Kvale and Brinkmann, 2009). However, when group rapport and trust cannot be established, the data collection will be too compromised to be of value. Trust involves both the group members and people outside the session. Being aware of ongoing relationships for members who expect to have continued contact after the focus group session is important. Issues of trust may arise owing to the sensitive nature of the topic, the vulnerability of the population, and/or concerns with the confidentiality of the data.

Other Purposes, Other Approaches

Other approaches to gathering qualitative information, not discussed in this book, include (Vande, Ven, and Delbecq, 1974):

- *Nominal Group Technique*, a process of reaching agreement by the anonymous generation of ideas in writing, round-robin recording of ideas, serial discussion to clarify ideas, and anonymous voting
- *Delphi*, a method that uses judgments of experts to obtain consensus on a topic by employing rounds of questionnaires for which experts provide anonymous opinions or by a multiple iteration survey technique that avoids the possible negative effects of group-dynamics brainstorming, which encourages creativity without regard for application
- *Discussion groups*, which can have various purposes, including education, consensus building, and support

These methods are distinct from the focus group approach, which is intended as a data-collection technique that utilizes the group interaction to enhance the quality of the data elicited.

Virtual Groups

Computers began to be used in a limited manner in the mid-1960s to analyze text data (Tesch, 1991). As technology advances, researchers continue to explore the possible advantages of using telephone-, Internet-, and computer approaches. There is agreement on the obvious advantages of these technologies, which include access to study participants in remote areas and to persons who may be reluctant to join a face-to-face meeting because of physical problems; possible reduced cost of arranging sessions; potentially increased disclosure as the result of perceived anonymity (this varies with topic and population); possibly more open responses; and real-time capture of data (Ayling and Mewse, 2009; Fox, Morris, and Rumsey, 2007; Franklin and Lowry, 2001; Frazier et al., 2010; Schneider et al., 2002; Stewart and Williams, 2005; Underhill and Olmsted, 2003; Valaitis and Sword, 2005; Walston and Lissitz, 2000).

The Internet is a medium that cannot be used in a simple manner by the researcher (James and Bushner, 2009); contexts need to be planned to take advantage of its potential. Because this medium is useful for people who are comfortable with online communication, its use will likely expand. Disadvantages of online sessions may include comment depth limited by lack of synchronicity in communication, absence of nonverbal cues, and/or level of typing ability. (Typing thoughts is more demanding than speaking them and may lead to a reduction in participation. However, using punctuation symbols and emoticons to express emotions can somewhat help participants to interpret text.)

All of these can be factors in the degree of content richness that participants can provide. Online communication limits the opportunity for the session facilitator to guide the discussion and follow up on questions. There is increased complexity of the issue of data security as well as possible misunderstanding of comments because of difficulty of establishing trust and rapport. In a synchronous session, a delay between responses may lead to reduced interaction and less synergy. Thus technology may, but not necessarily will, somewhat limit free communication (Morgan, Fellows, and Guevara, 2008).

Phone sessions have fewer disadvantages because of the perception of increased social cohesion—participants are able to use information from the real-time voice—but they still lack behavioral nonverbal cues.

Published articles that compare face-to-face and online groups by counting the number of utterances or words (Schneider et al., 2002; Underhill and Olmsted, 2003; Wutich et al., 2010), as contrasted with exploring meanings, are excluded from discussion here, because we focus on the collection of rich data, not the number of occurrences. If the purpose is to study how much interaction has occurred, a counting approach could be reasonable.

In general, online data collection may be somewhat constrained: group interaction will be less, and data will be less rich and deep. However, adaptations could be made to enhance online group interaction, such as small group size, previous face-to-face contact to establish rapport, and extra effort to describe the study and how data will be stored. And a sensitive or moderately sensitive topic may be more openly discussed online owing to a possibly increased comfort level resulting from some degree of anonymity. If the study's purpose can be met, the online approach might be preferred.

Mixed/Integrated Methods

The complexities of some topics in social science research and the limitations of some approaches may call for a combination of methods. Focus groups, as well as other qualitative approaches, have often been used to identify and explore the major concerns (domains of interest) in a topic that is new or not well understood. The natural vocabulary of participants can be used in the development of items for a questionnaire. In addition, when a researcher is using a well-established questionnaire in a population different from the population where it was developed, the meaning of items may need to be explored. The earlier somewhat adversarial relationship (Datta, 1994) between qualitative and quantitative approaches has generally dissipated. Planning and research design can balance the strengths and weaknesses of the qualitative and quantitative approaches. Morse and Niehaus (2009) present a very useful framework that can be used in designing multimethod projects.

Qualitative approaches have been used in combination with quantitative approaches in sequence or concurrently to reinforce, explain, or expand the data. *Reinforcement* is defined as using concurrent findings from two methods or two sources to support confidence in research findings, a process referred to as *triangulation*. To help explain quantitative results, focus groups have been used to understand the unanticipated or unexpected results of quantitative studies when well-established psychosocial instruments were used with a new population (Carey and Smith, 1992). Qualitative methods have also been used to explore the processes that underlie quantitative outcomes and to further develop the knowledge domain.

Rigor

Preparation must include strategies for ensuring rigor, which is usually understood as using the appropriate tools to address the stated objectives. As Morse and associates (2002) state, "without rigor, research is worthless, becomes fiction, and loses its utility." Although some stories appear persuasive and tug at the heart strings and might affect policy decisions, stories alone are not research. Rather than being a good source of credible information, they may instead be excellent theater. Although a vivid example drawn from solid research can be an excellent format to communicate results, decisions informed by the results must be based on solid information, not emotional responses. Because research influences policy decisions and resource allocations, it must be more than merely moving; to be useful, it must be rigorous and credible.

Focus group research designs must include strategies to evaluate the trustworthiness of the information gathered and the findings generated. Each stage of the research process must follow strategies for implementing rigor. These may include verification strategies that combine qualitative and quantitative methods or use various qualitative methods. Adequate documentation of the steps in the process of moving from data to findings is necessary to allow the reader to evaluate the credibility and usefulness of the findings. (Later chapters include some guidance in this area.)

Ethics

Although there are no published studies on the stress involved in being in a focus group, the literature on stress in other qualitative methods is informative. Corbin and Morse (2003) have found that the level of distress in interviews is no greater than in everyday life. In addition, there are many reports of therapeutic effects of being interviewed (Corbin and Morse, 2003; Kvale, 1996). However, for very sensitive topics and for some studies with people with special needs, the focus group facilitator needs skills to monitor the level of discomfort or distress. In addition, arrangements for referral for readily available support services may need to be established.

Payment and other incentives to participate need to be planned with the target population in mind. What is appealing to some could be coercive to others, especially for vulnerable populations.

Criticisms

Criticisms common to many qualitative studies include the topics of limited representativeness of sample, questionable validity of results, limited generalizability, lack of synthesis or under-analyzed findings, and inadequate documentation of process (audit trail). These concerns are addressed in basic qualitative research books (for example, Bogdan and Biklen, 2007; Hammersley and Atkinson, 1995; Mayan, 2009). Although this book provides some guidance to address these issues, it emphasizes the issues that are unique to the use of focus groups.

Concerns unique to focus groups include limited data quality, difficulty of data analysis, and ethical challenges. (The following chapters address these topics in more detail.) Data quality will be limited if the session is dominated by one or two people. When such domination occurs, it usually involves a variation in power or status, such as gender or professional status. Sometimes the facilitator's skill is not well enough developed to intervene effectively, although in rare circumstances there may be a limit on how effective any facilitator can be. Planning to have compatible members and obtaining group facilitator training with feedback on performance can help facilitators to deal with this problem.

Some criticisms arise from activities that are called focus groups, but on close inspection these groups do not actually meet the commonly accepted definition. One example is using a focus group in place of a survey to quickly gather data from many people at once. This use indicates a misunderstanding of the potential of the focus group method; using an actual survey in this case may be more appropriate, because rich data cannot be collected in a large group, and there would not be adequate time for many individual questions. Another misuse of the term *focus group* is for conducting a focus group in place of separate individual interviews. Having people come together and having a focus are not sufficient to be a focus group; such a gathering could be a class session or a football game. (Chapter 2 discusses the conceptual underpinnings of the group context, and Chapter 3 reviews how to appropriately use the focus group method.)

The collection of only brief comments—snippets—can result if the size of the group is large and time is too limited to collect detailed stories. When the goal is the collection of rich data, planning needs to include adequate time for each member to speak (face time)—especially for people who are not used to being in groups and are therefore less experienced or less comfortable speaking before a group. In addition, the number of questions needs to be limited in order to have time for discussion. (Group size and guideline-question development are discussed in later chapters.)

A few authors have described focus group sessions as chaotic and unwieldy (Kvale, 1996; Warr, 2005). However, this problem is not inherent in the method, and such sessions would lead to very questionable data and probably a poor use of time and expenses. Proper planning for a match of topic and group size, and adequate facilitator preparation, should preclude this problem. Infrequently a group session just does not come together well, and the reasons may not be determined; plans may need to be adjusted and other research approaches considered.

Analysis is the most underdeveloped component of the focus group technique. In addition to following the methods of the selected approach (such as grounded theory or thematic analysis), incorporating the effects of being in a group is essential in understanding the data; the two are not separable. (In later chapters, we explore a range of common analytic approaches and provide an example to two commonly used approaches.)

Ethical concerns are generally not a problem with sensitive topics. There is some evidence that, in some populations, some taboo topics are better explored in a group setting (Kitzinger, 1994). (The inadvertent self-disclosure of more than a member intended to reveal [*internal confidentiality*, Tolich, 2009] is addressed in a later chapter.)

Overall, careful planning and monitoring can address virtually all the criticisms of the focus group method. The potential usefulness of the findings far outweighs the effort and possible limitations.

Case Example

The research literature contains many examples of in-depth analysis using focus group data. In addition, there are very useful studies at a more descriptive level. Carley (1990, in Miles and Huberman, 1994) presents a model of levels of abstraction that covers a range of intensity. The first level consists of summarizing the data—conducting synopses and coding; the second level is identifying themes and searching for relationships; and the third level is developing and testing hypotheses or developing an explanatory framework. A focus group study may be designed to address any of these levels, and the intensity of analysis will be based on the purpose of the study.

Throughout this book, we use one of our own studies as an example, one that would fit in the second level, that of searching for themes (Asbury and Carey, 2005). We used focus groups with children as part of a larger study to assess the needs of high-risk children and to evaluate whether community prevention programs were meeting these needs. Community leaders and parents also participated in focus groups, separate from the children and teens. Boys and girls from grade school through high school age were considered at risk for developing future deviant behavior based on three factors: low academic achievement, low neighborhood attachment, and family conflict. This study used focus groups to elicit the unspoken and hard-to-articulate beliefs, challenges, and hopes of the youth. A local social service agency whose mission targeted families in need wanted to assess the children's needs, discover what would lead the children down the wrong path, and assess how well the existing programs were meeting these children's needs. The agency had previously attempted to survey students through the public school system but were not granted permission by the school system.

Our example is adapted from sessions that included 7 girls and boys, ages 6–11 years, in an after-school homework assistance setting. The group facilitator (Asbury), who had experience working with children, was assisted by a college-age assistant. The focus group setting was especially helpful in encouraging the dialogue necessary to explore the needs at a deep level.

Summary

Focus groups can be a very effective way of collecting rich, useful data. This approach capitalizes on the synergy of a group to elicit insights into the attitudes and beliefs that underlie behaviors. This chapter presents the basics of the focus group technique as used in social science research studies. In the next chapter we expand on this foundation by presenting the psychosocial framework that underlies the focus group method. We address concepts of constructing meaning, group dynamics, and reflectivity along with rigor, ethics, and criticisms.

2. Psychosocial Foundations

To use the strengths of focus groups and to adapt them to unique settings and populations with special needs, one must understand the conceptual framework that informs the focus group method. This chapter presents the concepts of constructing meaning, group dynamics, and reflectivity.

Key Questions

2.1. What is the "group effect," and why is it important to pay attention to it?

2.2. What ethical concerns are unique to focus groups and are not shared by other qualitative techniques?

Constructing Meaning

Human beings construct meaning by thinking about their experiences; they seek meaning by interpreting their environment, including people, in a dynamic process (Bruner, 1990). Concepts from symbolic interaction are useful in understanding this process of constructing meaning. Language involves shared meanings or symbols that contribute to understanding, and human behavior needs to be understood in a context of social interaction (Blumer, 1969; Mead, 1934). Meaning is personal and cultural, integrates the past and the present, and anticipates the future. Therefore, meaning always develops within a context, and so focus group data need to be understood within the context of the immediate environment of the session and the larger society.

Focus Group Research by Martha-Ann Carey and Jo-Ellen Asbury, 27–36 © 2012 Left Coast Press, Inc. All rights reserved.

A focus group session has elements in common with an individual interview in that the group facilitator and members "co-construct" the data in a way similar to that done by an interviewer and an interviewee, as described by Kvale and Brinkmann (2009). Together the interviewer and the interviewee develop an understanding of the interviewee's experience. This process is also true in a group setting, as the members, and to a lesser degree the facilitator, respond to one another.

Personal meanings and opinions also can be developed or shaped during a focus group session; this applies especially when a belief or an opinion was not well formed before session. A question for the researcher and the facilitator, therefore, is how to interpret changes in comments made by a member during a session. What led to these changes? This process of interpretation often is not straightforward, and the facilitator needs to carefully explore changes in comments from group members. (Exploring inconsistent comments is further discussed in later chapters on implementing focus groups and on working with special populations.)

Group Dynamics

Group interaction is both the strength and the potential limitation of the focus group technique. Members in a group session are interactive contributors of information. In addition to making meaning of experiences by independently reflecting on their own experiences, members participate within a social context, and they are affected by personal needs, previous experience with groups, facilitator skills, and the evolving group chemistry.

The group interaction capitalizes on *synergy* (from the Greek *synergos*, "working together"), whereby the whole is more than the sum of the individual parts, as the Gestalt psychologists have often noted (Wertheimer, 1928). People usually enjoy talking in a comfortable environment, and one story usually leads to another—a similar story or a different story. The flow of the stories may not follow the researcher's plan for the session. (How, why, and when the facilitator chooses to "go with the flow" are discussed in a later chapter.) Rich details are elicited by the interaction, and the members query one another about details as they try to understand and relate to one another. Highly articulate members who have experience with speaking in group settings may readily share their experiences and ideas. However, persons who have little or no experience in groups may be reticent to speak, at least initially. It is the responsibility of the facilitator to guide the discussion, as described in later chapters.

A group facilitator must be aware that factors that can affect participation occur on the social as well as the individual level. On the social level, issues of social dominance can inhibit participation. Characteristics that generally affect perceptions of social dominance include wealth, professional status, age, gender, ethnicity, and disability. Individual characteristics that affect participation include need for approval, experience with topic, trust, and self-esteem (Carey, 1994). Other individual factors include commitment to one's publicly expressed opinion, affiliation need, concern for being evaluated, and need for social comparison (Hastie, 1986). However, the common experience of the study topic may override the influence of these characteristics. In a very early HIV study with active-duty U.S. military, we found that the experience of being diagnosed with HIV overrode the social differentiation due to rank for enlisted men and officers, and we combined these personnel in sessions (Carey and Smith, 1992). The interactions in focus groups held for members from the three service branches were very productive in collecting information to inform the refinement of the research protocol.

Often a de facto power asymmetry exists between the facilitator and the group members (Karnielli-Miller, Strier, and Pessach, 2009; Kvale, 2006). Generally, the researcher and/or the facilitator develops the discussion questions, and the facilitator leads the discussion. (More recently, there has been more participation by the target population in all phases of a study.) However, the usual asymmetry, especially with a highly structured session, could lead to the dialogue being somewhat one-way between each member and the facilitator. Synergy will be limited, and a diminished richness of data will result. Some settings inherently have an unequal power distribution, such as Carey and Smith's (1992) work with the U.S. military. This situation was addressed by having nonmilitary persons conduct the focus groups; the facilitator had a clinical (nursing) background, the co-facilitator had previous military experience, and the sessions were held off-site. (Suggestions for planning and implementing sessions are discussed in later chapters.)

The quality of the group interaction, and subsequently the quality of the data, is enhanced by the establishment of rapport and trust. The group members must feel that they are respected and that they are valued as experts in their experiences. This situation is enhanced by the group facilitator having some knowledge of the topic and of the population from which the group members are drawn; it is difficult for the facilitator to explore the depth and richness of the data without truly understanding what is being said. Although the facilitator may need to begin with little knowledge if there is very little known about the topic, learning as the research progresses will lead to richer data collection. In addition, the group leader needs to be respected as a legitimate person to lead the group—one who is capable of leading a group session and who has the ability to listen and understand.

Potential limitations to participation may include the results of *self-censoring* (Janis, 1972) or *conforming* (Asch, 1951). Self-censoring occurs when a member is influenced by his or her perception of what the group expects (particularly in cases in which future interaction with the group members is expected) and chooses not to share a conflicting experience. This decision may be due to lack of trust in the group facilitator or the members or to concern about future uses of the data. Conforming may involve stating agreement with the comments expressed by the group members, even though their comments are not truly believed, or may be a process of cognitive restructuring that can occur when a member's opinion is influenced by other members (Festinger, 1957). Psychosocial experiments involving group work have shown that having just one ally, defined as someone who agrees with you or who differs from the majority, can be enough support for the member to speak up with information that differs from the majority opinion (Asch, 1951). The facilitator must be able to distinguish, as far as possible, what is occurring, because he or she will follow up or probe—or do nothing—depending on what events are occurring. (Conducting a session is discussed in Chapter 4.)

We now turn to examples from our study to illustrate the processes of self-censoring and conforming. The examples of transcript have been modified from the study described earlier (Asbury and Carey, 2005). The transcript has been adapted to provide highlights of different aspects of using focus groups. Names have been changed. Participants' names are Brad (age 9), Sasha (age 6), Ian (age 7), Caren (age 8), Michael (age 9), and Jose (age 8). Some knew the others, and some did not.

Example 1: Self-Censoring

Facilitator: Do you know people about your age who have tried alcohol? Drinking?

Brad: Yes.

Sasha: Some boy brought stuff to school.

Facilitator: Somebody who's about your age?

Sasha: Yes

Caren: I did one thing . . . kinda like smoking, but I don't want to say because people here go to my school.

It is clear from this short discussion that Caren was not comfortable with sharing the details, because she realized that her behavior was not acceptable to some of the others in the group, and she would have continued contact with some of them. In some circumstances, the facilitator would choose to try to further explore her comments. However, the girl seemed uncomfortable, and the facilitator chose to move on to other comments.

Example 2: Conforming—Going along with the Group

Facilitator: What would you do if someone tried to get you to do something that you don't want to do?

Brad: I'd yell "No" and walk away.

Michael: Yeah, I'd walk away.

Jose: It depends I guess . . . on how who the person is. If it is a friend, I'd just say "No," but if it was a stranger or an older person, I'd run away.

Michael: I'm not sure.

[Ian has been silent to this point, but is fidgeting in his chair and looks a bit uncomfortable.]

Facilitator: Any other ideas?

Ian: Well . . . I'd go tell an adult.

Brad: Aww, man . . . would you really do that?

[Ian, looks uncertain.]

Ian: Well, maybe not. I guess I'd walk away.

In this example, Ian's second comment is a change from his first comment. It is quite possible that he would like to tell an adult in that situation, but Brad's comment has led to Ian saying maybe he would not. The group facilitator would follow up on this and try to come back to Ian later in the session, with some support for a range of options. If Ian stays with the second comment, the data would clearly be questionable.

Example 3: Conformity—Opinion Change

Facilitator: If you had the chance, would you try a cigarette?

[The children look at one another (nervously?) and laugh.]

Jose: I had a friend who tried a cigarette.

Facilitator: Really?

Jose: Yes, but he was a bigger kid.

Brad: My dad smokes.

Facilitator: Does he smoke in the house?

Brad: No.

Michael: If someone one offered me a cigarette, I'd try it if I wouldn't get caught.

[Some boys laugh.]

Jose: Yeah, I would too.

Ian: Me too.

Facilitator: Do you think most of your friends would try it?

Bonnie: I wouldn't. Smoking is bad for you. My uncle had to quit when he got emphysema.

Ian: Yeah, it is bad for you.

Michael: Yeah, I probably wouldn't try it. It's dumb.

Michael's first and second comments do not agree. Bonnie's statement has led to Michael's second comment, which seems to imply a possible change in his attitude, as contrasted with merely saying something he does not believe. The comment "*it's dumb*" seems to suggest that Michael may be trying to make up his mind. The facilitator would further explore what the children understand of the danger and what they might do.

The facilitator should be skilled in recognizing possible limitations and, as far as possible, in minimizing them, a discussion we take up in a later chapter. The facilitator can ameliorate, to an extent, these potentially troublesome social-influence effects by following suggestions from Merton, Fiske, and Kendall (1990), which are informed by basic social psychology concepts. The four characteristics that Merton and colleagues described as important in eliciting useful information are depth, personal context, range, and specificity. For example, the facilitator asks the group members to "think back" to their experience. This helps to place to the discussion in the context of the experience and brings to mind rich details. Next, the facilitator explores with the group the range and breath of experiences, as appropriate to the study topic. The facilitator's aim is to explore the personal context by eliciting detailed, specific, and personal information. If a group member wishes to describe a friend's experiences, especially relative to a problematic area, we encourage such stories. It may be fairly clear that the "friend's" story is probably actually the group member's, but that person may feel safer commenting in an less personal manner. This approach may be the best alternative to disclosing actual personal details.

Formerly, focus group sessions were planned so that members did not know one another and did not expect to have further contact. More recently, however, group sessions are formed with members from existing social units, which has both advantages and disadvantages. It is apparent that when members know one another, they likely have language in common, which can facilitate communication. However, trust is not necessarily stronger in these groups, because members may be reluctant to disclose information when they know that they will have continued contact with other members.

Tolich (2009) describes the diminished autonomy resulting from connected relationships. This effect is less clear with children who know one another, because they are more likely than adults to trust their peers (Morgan et al., 2002). Having friends helps them to speak up. However, that might not be helpful if they do not want to speak publicly when the topic involves blame, shame, or fault. Age and gender are also factors in the children's contributions (Morgan et al., 2002). There may be more posturing and macho-like behavior for adolescent boys, and more bonding for girls.

Some studies ask people to write down their opinions before a session in order to ameliorate the effect of the group swaying their opinions and to lessen the potential effects of censoring or conformity. Because some group members may not come to the session with well formed opinions, the writing process may solidify their opinions. In addition, this process could lead to less group interaction and synergy and possibly diminish the richness of elicited data, because people may feel that they should defend their written opinions, which could lead to conflict or competition. Studies in cognitive dissonance have found that when people have committed to an idea, they are less likely to be open to new information (Festinger, 1957). People may be biased in thinking that their opinions are correct, despite any conflicting information.

Factors to consider in having group members write down their opinions before the session begins include the researcher's expectations about how willing and able members would be to resist group effects and how the study purpose in exploring previously unformed opinions would be served. The ambiguity of the task, the sensitivity of the topic, and personality traits are additional factors. Overall, it is usually better not to have opinions written down before a session; group synergy is the key factor, and it will be less effective when members feel a need to defend their written comments.

Reflectivity

Qualitative researchers are encouraged to be *reflective*. A simple definition of this term is "to be thoughtful and insightful." In the context of qualitative research, being reflective refers to a turning in, or being self-reflective, in order to observe our own understandings and bias. We cannot move away from our social world so that we can impartially study a topic (Hammersley and Atkinson, 1995). Our historic and sociocultural position, our values and needs, are part of the lens through which we observe, interpret, and make meaning in life. More broadly, the research process of interviewing, probing for clarity, and co-constructing data may influence the data collected (Hall and Callery, 2001). When the research report includes adequate details of the research process and the reflective process, the reader can judge the quality of the data collected and the analysis process.

We plan our studies to take into account the perspectives we bring. Interviews with our professional peers can help to make us aware of our perspectives—when the research is being planned and during the study, as well as at the end of data collection and during analysis. Being reflective is especially important for qualitative focus group work, because the data are co-constructed and the researchers' perspectives will influence the data.

An excellent example is the reflective process that was an important part of Anne Odell's (2008) grounded theory research with a Hawaiian community. Odell had lived in the Hawaiian community many years ago and maintained family contacts there. She had some clear opinions about political and health care delivery issues for this community, and she had questions about the elders' (*Kūpuna*) understanding of health and wellness. Odell met with her three advisors before, during, and after data collection and analysis to clarify her expectations and identify bias. She did not set aside her knowledge—as is described in some phenomenology studies as "bracketing"; rather she used her knowledge to understand the data. With guidance from her advisors, she was able to identify where she was coming from and how that could affect her understanding of the data. She had a special responsibility to ground in the data each code, the development of the categories, the themes, and the model. When she later took the findings back to the *Kūpuna*, she found a grateful reception. They appreciated the opportunity to contribute, enjoyed being in the focus groups, and were pleased that the findings reflected their own life experiences.

Rigor

The term *validation* is often used in connection with data and also may be used to examine the process of the study. For qualitative studies, rigor is essential to the construction of knowledge, and it is not determined by applying a fixed set of rules. It is best examined by exploring the sources of potential bias and is a concept to be addressed throughout the research process (Kvale, 1995; Morse et al., 2002). Good research design needs to be flexible to address emerging potential confounds. (This need is discussed in the following chapters.)

Ethics

Increasing attention has been devoted to the protection of participants in research. Certain requirements must be formally addressed in most research settings—for example, approval by the ethics board of an organization, professional organizations' standards, and local requirements. Also, research supporters and parent organizations may have their own ethical requirements as well as other concerns. No one set of ethical guidelines can be used as a checklist. And the general principles of respect, beneficence, and justice need to be woven into every element of the focus group research method (Smith, 1995; Tolich, 2009). In addition, there generally are legally required reporting issues, such as child abuse and other intent to harm. (Note that these requirements vary by country and within countries.) The researcher needs to explain to the group members that such data cannot be kept confidential. Of course, making participants aware of such requirements will likely lead to some self-censoring, as would be appropriate. Participants' wishes on the release of findings need to be respected and should be negotiated at an early stage.

Throughout this book, we highlight other ethical concerns.

Summary

By understanding the psychosocial foundations of focus groups, the researcher can appreciate the complexity of data that are collected in a group setting. The most important theoretical issues are how meaning is co-constructed in a group setting, the potential effects—both positive and negative—of group interaction, and the importance of being reflective. These theoretical understandings will assist the researcher in planning the study and analyzing the data. The quality of evidence will be enhanced, and therefore the evidence will be more useful for policy and practice.

In Chapter 3 we move into a detailed discussion of the process of planning focus group sessions. We discuss not only what must be considered and done before the sessions but also how addressing these issues can enhance rigor and uphold research ethics.

3. Planning

Careful planning is crucial for the obtaining the best-quality data. This chapter is divided into an overview and topics to be considered in planning for before, during, and after focus group sessions.

Key Questions

3.1. What is "internal confidentiality," and how can a facilitator plan to address it?

3.2. What is the relationship between "probing" and data quality?

3.3. What are the unique characteristics of your target population that need to be addressed in planning?

3.4. How will you address the issues of rigor and data credibility?

Overview

Research can be only as useful as the quality of the data and the analysis. Planning is like a pipeline: early restrictions or limitations from inadequate planning cannot be remedied by increased attention later. This phase is crucial and merits time and attention; often, more time is needed than anticipated to think through the topic and the activities. In addition, the quality of the data is dependent on the development of trust of the participants, and therefore careful planning requires attention to clear communication of the purpose of the study, how the data will be handled, and how the results will be reported. Overall, the design should reflect the coherence between purpose (goal), process (sampling and analysis), and product (findings or results).

Focus Group Research by Martha-Ann Carey and Jo-Ellen Asbury, 37–58 © 2012 Left Coast Press, Inc. All rights reserved.

Considerations in designing a study include who will use the information and to what purpose. And preparing for publications and presentations should start in the planning stage.

Before the Session

Planning elements to be considered before the session include consent, transcription and translation, facilitator preparation, co-facilitator roles, sampling, recruitment, group size, and preparation of a checklist.

As in all research, the research question is framed within the context of resources, which include time, finances, expertise, equipment, and access to the population. Usually one works with colleagues or assistants, perhaps on mutually beneficial and possibly complementary projects. Planning should include development of agreement on roles and responsibilities, and possible changes across the phases of the project. Availability is as important as having expertise. Expectations should be spelled out as clearly as possible and updated regularly. Who will have access to data for publication and when should be established early on. When the team includes community members, these members may benefit from some training in the process of research in general as well as specifics of the current project. For example, much of U.S. government funding requires that data be shared, after identifying information has been removed.

Involving the research participants in planning, as well as other phases, can be very informative. Incorporating input from as many stakeholders involved in the research as practical is more likely to produce findings of practical use, because the findings will more authentically reflect the social context of the participants. Clarifying roles and responsibilities is especially important for participatory research when members from the population of interest are partners as full members of the team. Participants have rich knowledge of the topic, and researchers generally do not have the life experience of the research topic. Each group needs to listen to and respect the knowledge and limits of the other. It is common for researchers to try to incorporate community members in planning, but less often are the needs of researchers (especially funding requirements) adequately explained to the community research partners.

Consent

Some aspects of ethics are unique to focus groups, and particular problems may arise from the group setting. For example, the synergistic effect of being in a lively group setting may lead to more disclosure than a group member intended (Carey, 1994; Smith, 1995; Tolich, 2009). Tolich has called this aspect "internal confidentiality"; it includes the problem of a group member not being able to take back or "erase" a comment, which would be possible in an interview format. Tolich recommends that the consent form include a description of limitations.

Some aspects of maintaining confidentiality of data go beyond the control of the researcher in that there are limits on what level of confidentiality can be maintained. For example, it is impossible for the group facilitator to guarantee "What is said here, stays here." The group facilitator can be responsible only for her or his own actions, not the actions of the other group members. This is especially a concern when the topic of the focus group may include painful experiences.

Transcription and Translation

A somewhat common misperception is that verbatim transcripts are completely accurate records of what occurred during the session. Transcription necessarily removes some of the richness of the data in the session. In discussing constructing versus reproducing, Hammersley (2010) warns that transcriptions are not representations of sounds recorded but rather of words heard. In addition to possibly not being accurate records, transcripts generally do not include tone of voice, gestures, and other nonverbal forms of communication. Poland (1995) argues that capturing the emotional context is necessary. Field notes, especially notes on nonverbal communication and group interaction, are essential to understanding the data. Video recordings help to address this concern.

In the case of audio recording, members' comments may overlap and not be recorded clearly. The facilitator is usually able to guide the discussion so that this should only rarely be a problem—when members are requested to speak one at a time. Another problem is identifying who is speaking—information that is needed to follow the consistency of each member's comments. When the facilitator is involved in the transcription, or when she or he reads the transcripts promptly after the session and listens to the tapes while reading the transcript, identification problems will be minimized.

Selection of the type of transcription varies with purpose and resources. One approach, performed immediately after the session, is not an actual transcript but rather descriptive notes of what the group facilitator determines to be the important concepts, made immediately after the session. This "top of the line" approach is like an art form and can be useful in a marketing type of study, but it is seldom useful in behavioral science research. Another approach—one that conditions sometimes require—is to use notes only. Such conditions include scarcity of resources, limited scope of the project, or short turn-around time. A third approach is abstracted text, created when one listens to the audio recordings or watches the video and writes down the important or salient parts. This approach can be especially useful for preliminary analysis before planning a next step.

These approaches provide only limited data; in-depth analysis generally requires verbatim transcript. This is the standard approach and can be considered necessary in order to be rigorous. When doing line-by-line coding (explained below), this type of transcript is necessary.

Another challenge arises when the sessions are conducted in a language other than one understood well by the researcher. A previously held model is that the interpretation/translation process is passive and mechanical, whereas a new model involves the co-construct of knowledge (Edwards, 1998). In a somewhat similar concept to Kvale's (1995) description of the co-construction of information in an interview, Larkin and de Casterle (2007) describe the interpreter as co-constructing information, and this interpretation is appropriate in translating for meaning as contrasted with the word-for-word approach. In this sense, the interpreter is participating in the research. This role needs to be made explicit, and the interpreter should be included in the analysis and understanding of the findings (Shklarov, 2007). This is especially true when the study involves sensitive data from vulnerable populations.

Wong and Poon (2010) highlight both the potentially powerful role of the interpreter/translator in cross-cultural research and the reality that not just any bilingual individual can be effective in interpreting/translating. Wong and Poon's research found that when there is not a clear cultural equivalent of a word or an expression, interpreters must use their own understanding of the meaning, according to their own experiences. Wong and Poon found significant variations in translations. In addition to being unfamiliar with the variations of subcultures, an individual who long ago left her native land may not be fluent in the current cultural nuances. For example, within a mainstream ethnic and socioeconomic setting, limited understanding of meaning is clearly seen in the rapid changes in the meanings of fads in the youth culture.

Facilitator Preparation

Appropriate preparation of the group facilitator greatly assists the smooth running of the session. In addition to a literature review (which is limited in the early stages for most qualitative work), in order to plan for recruitment, conduct the session, and explore stories as they emerge, the facilitator must have some knowledge of the people and the topic. She or he needs to understand comments in relation to slang and local context. For example, in the gay culture a "sister" is a close colleague, not a sibling. This term describes a personal and usually supportive relationship, not a biological fact. A teenager may state that some idea or presentation is "tight," which means it is very desirable and up-to-date. Logistics should be organized in advance so that details, such as of the setup of the room and the provision of food, do not distract the facilitator, and he or she can maintain as alert and calm a mental posture as possible. A calm mental state is an asset for the intense job of processing comments and group interactions during the session.

Co-Facilitator Roles

Most focus groups include a co-facilitator to assist the facilitator. This is especially advisable when the group facilitator is new to guiding group sessions, when the number of people in each session is large (greater than seven), or when the topic is complex or very sensitive. The co-facilitator assists with the logistics, especially the recording and room arrangements. Common "host" duties include seeing that food is available, escorting late arriving members to the session, providing directions to the bathrooms, taking messages, and providing a contact for members when cell phones and pagers are turned off.

The most important functions are taking notes on nonverbal communication as it relates to the spoken comments, noting the group interaction, helping the facilitator to monitor that the guideline questions are addressed, and summarizing at the end of the session. A person who is new to running group sessions and who wishes to learn to be a session facilitator can fill this role.

Sampling

Members are recruited based on their common experience with the topic. As is the case with most qualitative studies, this purposive sampling is intended to explore the topic, not to be representative of the population in a statistical sense. The design may include planning for group members to represent a range of experiences across the topic, or it may focus more narrowly for greater depth. The most unique cases, sometimes called deviant cases, can provide very useful data (Patton, 2002). In addition to having experience with the topic, characteristics desired in an interviewee include being available and willing to participate, and being articulate and reflective (Spradley, 1979).

Generally, members are homogenous in terms of prestige or status, such as occupation, social class, age, and education. Such homogeneity is often useful, because people are more likely to share information with others whom they see as similar. If the group is too heterogeneous, however, the lower status members will likely defer to higher status members and not contribute fully. (Although, as we mentioned earlier, Carey [1994] found that in working with a military population, the common experience of having HIV or AIDS overcame the demographic differences in rank.)

For later use in reporting and analysis, the researcher should record the inclusion and exclusion criteria, the recruitment process (how recruitment was done, how many agreed to participate), the number of members per session, and the number of sessions. In addition, she or he should document the setting of sessions as well as the length and characteristics of group interactions, and note if members were assigned to sessions based on characteristics such as demographic variables.

For some studies, the researcher may choose to include in the same session people with different roles, such as teachers and parents. When experiences from different perspectives are shared in this type of group, the discussion can be more informative than having separate groups. However, caution is advised in using this approach, because conflicts may arise that could detract from data collection. A pilot may be useful to explore the effectiveness of this arrangement.

Previously, focus groups usually consisted of strangers who expected not to have future contact. It is now becoming more common for members to know one another and to expect to have future contact. This familiarity has important consequences for the data quality; members may be more reticent to share when power differentials exist and sensitive topics are the focus. For example, wondering if your supervisor will hear about what you said in the group could easily lead to self-censored data. Knowing your fellow members, however, may lead to easier conversation.

Planning for the number of sessions will be guided by the study's purpose and scope, as well as the responses of the participants. For an exploratory project, there might be as few as three sessions with six members in each session. For a more in-depth study used in model building and theory development, several sessions likely would be needed to be able to examine fully the relationships and categories. Data saturation occurs when the newly collected information does not add to the knowledge and when the analysis does not need more information to flesh out the categories, as described in the next chapter. If session participation would be enhanced by dividing members into sessions by a characteristic such as socioeconomic status, it is recommended that more than one session be held per segment. The group dynamics will vary with each session, and what is responded to in one session may not arise in another session.

Recruitment

Recruitment often is a two-step process with the first invitation coming from an organization that has permission to contact the target population (see Box 3.1 for a sample recruitment letter). This invitation includes a brief description of the study and information for contacting the researcher. Next, the researcher contacts those who have agreed to participate, screening with exclusion and inclusion criteria if appropriate. The researcher provides additional information and arranges for a convenient time and place to conduct a session. Occasionally, the researcher may have permission to make the first contact and will need to explain how the person's name and contact information were obtained. In place of, or addition to a phone call, a follow-up letter is useful to confirm the contact; the purpose of the study and how the data will be handled should be included. A consent form may be included at this stage or at a later stage. The researcher should ask if there are special needs, such as food requirements or accommodations for hearing or other physical limitations. A reminder phone call the day or evening before the session is scheduled leads to lower rate of no-shows.

Incentives are described in the recruitment letter or other initial contact. Incentives may be needed more in focus group studies than in other studies, because participating in a scheduled session is more of a burden than is a phone interview or a questionnaire. The incentive is a token of appreciation for participation, and its selection reflects that the researcher understands what the participants would value. Money is often used, because it is immediately rewarding and is easily used by the participants; the amount needs to be large enough to be considered of value but not large enough to be coercive. For some people, contributing to the research appeals to their sense of altruism and is quite rewarding.

Box 3.1   Sample Recruitment Letter

The organization is the official sender, because the organization has access to the names and contact information. In most instances, until the participants or the legal representatives give permission, the researcher may not contact participants directly. The local organization generally will find it helpful to have been provided a draft letter.

<organization letterhead>

<date>

The Local Community Organization is reviewing its afterschool programs for young children to determine if the existing programs are meeting the needs of the children. Interviews and focus groups are planned with parents and children. We are writing to ask your permission for your child to participate in a 45-minute discussion within the next month, to be held at the Local Center during their normal after-school hours. Refreshments will be provided. The session will be tape-recorded, but names will be deleted. No identifying information will be disclosed. The group facilitator, Dr. Jo-Ellen Asbury from Local University, is a researcher with several years' experience as a teacher of young children. This is expected to be a fun experience for the children, and they will be given a ten-dollar certificate for a local restaurant.

If you grant permission for your child to participate, please fill out the enclosed postcard and mail it to me. Please contact me if you have any questions or want more information.

Sincerely,
Jane Doe
Local Community Director
555-123-4567

Recruitment processes may be less formal, as the setting requires. For example, the focus groups of heroin users in the methadone clinics in the south Bronx section of New York City (Carey and Langert-DeGori, 2000) necessitated in-person recruiting on the day of the session. Extra care was taken to ensure informed consent, because the time of consent and the session were close together and this was an especially vulnerable population.

Group Size

Recommendations in the research literature relative to group size vary from five to ten per session. We find groups larger than seven or eight a bit large and harder to manage. However, factors beyond the absolute numbers must be considered. A small number usually leads to greater depth of data, and small group size is especially important for sensitive, complex topics. Persons not used to sharing in groups will feel more comfortable with only three or four others, rather than eight to ten others. People need "face time" (their chance to talk) in order for the researcher to collect stories instead brief snippets, which are quick, superficial comments. Snippets may be appropriate for some work, but the purpose of using focus groups to get rich data generally cannot be met with snippets. However, a descriptive project could use a large group to obtain brief comments and then summarize the results. Factors to consider include the sensitivity and complexity of the topic, and the abilities, expectations, and needs of the group members.

With a small group, the facilitator can more easily manage the group dynamics, process the information, and attend to each member. The disadvantage is that conducting many small groups is more labor intensive, because data are collected from fewer people per session. However, the collection of better quality data, even though from fewer participants, is a wise choice in virtually any study.

A study may involve more than one session per group. This multiple-session format could be helpful when the topic is complex or when members have limited time to participate because of an illness or limited attention span. When multiple sessions are anticipated, the consent form should reflect this. The dynamics of the group may be different in multiple-session studies, because the group process will have time to develop more and members will work out more clearly the roles they take.

Checklist

With many details to remember, the researcher can use a checklist (Box 3.2) to aid in organization and concentration on obtaining the best quality of data. Checklists are especially helpful for researchers new to using focus groups. Because researchers' needs vary, the level of checklist detail will also vary and may be modified as the researchers and group facilitators gain experience. It may be useful to review some examples of checklists as you prepare your own list (Creswell, 2009; Krueger and Casey, 2009).

Box 3.2   Sample Checklist

Planning

Read about topic and population

Establish contact and get approvals

Letter of invitation

Follow-up letter for people who agree to participate, with details of session, check for special needs

Reminder phone call shortly before session

Before Session

Develop and test guideline questions

Consent form

Recording equipment—tape recorder, microphone, batteries or extension cords, tape for extension cord, extra tapes if appropriate

Name cards, pens

Facilitator and co-facilitator preparation, establish responsibilities, familiar with guideline questions

Arrange for room and food

During

Introduction to session

Contact information if needed

At end—incentives given to members

After

Check recording quality

Debrief—possibly on tape

During the Session

Planning items involved during the session include logistics, the introduction, guideline questions, probing, and facilitator style and session structure.

Logistics

Logistic details important to the successful use of focus groups include the room setting, recording procedures and equipment, and food and beverages. Details, such as the furniture arrangements, should be carefully considered. The room should be comfortable and afford privacy so that few interruptions will occur. Consideration may be given to holding the focus group off the organization's premises, away from the physical setting associated with the research topic, to provide a psychological break and thus possibly encourage sharing of information. Make notes of the differences in logistical settings among focus groups, because changes in circumstances may affect group members' participation. For example, a focus group held during lunch time may limit discussion or exploration of topics in depth if participants feel pressured by the time limitation.

Food is a surprisingly important aspect. In our experience, brownies were a hit with military personnel, bagels and coffee were appreciated by older citizens for a morning session in a senior center, and pizza went well with high school and college students. Food facilitates presession conversation and provides group members with something to do. This presession chatting, often around the food table, helps break the ice socially, but more important, it allows the facilitator to observe the members' characteristics and to arrange optimal seating.

The placement of individuals around a table can affect the dynamics of the group. For example, the facilitator could place an outspoken person close to her chair, so that the facilitator can better guide the level of participation of that member by turning toward or away from that person. Similarly, a shy or reticent person can be seated directly across from the facilitator allowing for eye contact and other nonverbal means of encouragement to participate. The co-facilitator may be seated back from the group in order to better observe.

Recording equipment should be thoroughly tested before the focus group session starts. Logistical details such as extension cords, duct tape to cover cords and wires, and extra batteries should be taken care of before the session and organized before the participants enter. The recording equipment should be arranged as unobtrusively as possible. After giving an introduction outlining the purpose of the research, the facilitator then asks permission to record the session, via audiotape or videotape. He or she explains the helpfulness of not having to take extensive notes and the desire to record the important details of each member's contributions. Although audiotape is more commonly used, videotaping allows the researcher to capture more of the nonverbal aspects of members' participation, which can be helpful in placing comments in context. However, videotaping of sessions requires more equipment and may be distracting to some members. If members object to the use of a tape recorder or other device, the facilitator can record the essence of the session using only notes, although with this method it is harder to get adequate data. Some situations may prohibit the use of audio or video recording, and the facilitator will have to rely on memory. This method requires skill and experience. Although it can be useful in marketing work, this technique should not be used for rigorous research unless necessary.

Some studies include use of a flip chart to record comments. Although it is reinforcing for a member to see his or her words written down, a possible consequence can be the expectation of consensus when such is not the goal. Writing on a flip chart or white board may help to remind very young group members of the rules, such as one person talking at a time.

Session Introduction

The welcome and introduction to the session are important to establish trust and an appropriate comfort level among the participants. Information about the project, expanded from the recruitment letter, includes the purpose of the study, which organization is supporting this project, and why the funding agency or supporting organization is interested in this work. Also described are how the data will be kept, who will have access, and who will transcribe or watch the video recording. This information should help to provide a level of comfort to the members and will encourage their participation. When warranted, the facilitator should describe any relevant reporting requirements, such as the legal requirement to report child abuse and danger to self or others. The participants may react to these statements by limiting their comments, as is appropriate. (As mentioned, the consent form should also include this information.)

The facilitator asks permission to tape (audio or video), as previously described in the recruitment letter. The facilitator explains that the recording process helps capture all the members' comments, asks that one person speak at a time, and states that no names will be included in any reports or publications. After receiving oral permission, the facilitator begins recording. The facilitator, or the researcher previously, generally offers to send a summary of the results and asks for contact information if the participants request this summary.

Part of the facilitator's introduction includes setting ground rules for discussion. Two very broad rules are these: only one person talks at a time, and there are no right answers. Generally, consensus is not the purpose, and the facilitator encourages a diversity of comments, emphasizing that there are no correct answers and that the facilitator expects a range of experiences. The introduction (Box 3.3) used in our example was tailored to the understanding of the young people in the session. Wording was at their developmental level, and appropriate phrasing was used.

Box 3.3 Sample Introduction

Before the tape recorder is turned on, the children are seated at the table after mingling around the food table. Paper and crayons are passed out, and an instruction is given to draw a picture of what they want to be in ten years.

Thanks for agreeing to be part of this group. I am Professor Asbury from Local University, and this is Susan, who will be helping me. She will be taking some notes, because sometimes it is hard for me to really listen to you and write at the same time.

Give out name tags and pens. Please write down your name—whatever name you wish and that's what I'll call you today.

As you draw your pictures of what you want to be in ten years, let's check out this tape recorder. Please say your name, and then I'll play it back for you. Please speak one at a time, and raise your hand if you want to get my attention. If too many speak at once, we can't make out the different voices on the tape.

Each child says his or her name, and then I play back the tape. This procedure helps them to get used to the taping and get comfortable with the group setting. The children enjoyed hearing their voices.

For some questions today, I may ask you about things your friends might do. Be sure to protect their names—try not to say their real names.

Are there any questions before we begin?

Today we are going to talk about what you want to be in ten years, and how you can get there.

Guideline Questions

Guideline questions provide some structure for the session. Questions are developed based on what is known and the purpose of the study. In our example (Box 3.4), the needs assessment project and the guideline questions were informed by the literature on risk and protective factors in preventing delinquent behavior in adolescents (Hawkins, Catalano, and Miller, 1992; Kumpfer and Alvarado, 2003). Be sure to spend adequate time trying out and refining these questions, preferably with pilot sessions. Documenting changes in guideline questions as the study progresses and explaining why the decisions were made are an important part of documenting the process of the study.

Box 3.4   Guideline Questions

1. When people say a kid is a bad kid, what do they mean?

   Think about the people you know, kids your age. What kinds of trouble do kids your age get into?

   Do you know anyone who smokes cigarettes? Has anyone tried alcohol?

   What about people suspended from school? Have any of you been suspended?

2. Tell me about your picture of what you want to be.

3. What do you need to do to get where you want to be? What would make a difference in having your dream come true?

In developing guideline questions, keep in mind the purpose of collecting rich data. Too many questions will lead to only superficial snippets or brief comments, which would be appropriate only if that is the goal of the study. In general, consider the four characteristics that Merton and colleagues (Merton, Kendall, and Fiske, 1990) described as key characteristics: depth, personal context, range, and specificity. The sessions should aim to get the depth of the personal experience—affect and values, detailed and vivid information is the goal. Personal context is needed to allow the researchers to interpret the data from each individual's perspective. The desired range of experiences is guided by the goal of the study, with a broad range the goal in most exploratory studies and a narrower range when some information is known. Aiming for specific details in the comments helps to ensure the quality of the data. Keeping these goals in mind, the facilitator would likely limit the number of guideline questions to three or four, with subquestions used to further explore each question.

The order of the guideline questions helps to structure the discussion by easing group members into a mindset to assist them in describing details of their opinions or experiences. One approach is to ask a very general question to get the group oriented to the topic and then to narrow the focus to a more specific aspect of the study. The session may not proceed as the facilitator anticipated in terms of the order of the questions, usually because of the interest of the members. As described in the next chapter, it is usually wise to recognize the interest of the group and follow their lead, because they likely are following what is most important to them.

In the Asbury and Carey (2005) example, the order of questions was unique; it was planned to get the children first thinking of actual and potential problems and next describing what they wanted to be—in a very abstract manner, as the data show. They then could consider what they needed to realize their dreams. This information likely could not have been obtained by a straightforward approach, and the group interaction clearly showed the synergy. The "opening question" is not of interest to the research itself and is called an "ice breaker." It is used only to get the group talking. Once someone has spoken, even in response to a simple question of fact such as "How old are you?" or "What clubs do you go to after school?" it is easier for that person to speak again. When planning for this question, a simple question of general interest that is easy to answer works best. In our example, Asbury asked the children to say their names and ages for recording.

Summarizing at the end of each question before moving on to the next question can be helpful to clarify highlights and to check if members are ready to move on. Summarizing is possible even if the discussion does not follow the guideline questions, because there may be some natural breaks or changes. At the end of the session, the co-facilitator can check that main ideas have been captured accurately. This process is member checking of data, not of analysis.

In addition to guideline questions, other techniques are helpful in eliciting data. Before the discussion begins, members may be asked to take photos, draw a picture, make a brief movie, or write a letter or a simple poem. Some researchers have used a vignette rather than guideline questions and asked members to respond to it (Brondani et al., 2008). The usefulness of the activity depends on the ability and interest of the participants.

In considering how useful or needed this approach can be, the researcher can consider if members will be likely to respond to the guideline questions and participate in the discussion. In addition to helping to establish rapport, such activities help to guide the discussion, assist the members to focus on the questions, help members to "think back," and make abstract concepts more concrete.

Such techniques are generally useful for young persons and people who are not used to being in groups. Producing drawings and writing about them is a common experience for most school-aged children. Asking children to describe their picture not only is a child friendly technique but also puts the child in the role of expert, possibly changing the balance of power by moving the focus from the facilitator to the child (Horstman et al., 2008).

When the researcher is not familiar with the members or the culture, it can be helpful to have such techniques readily available to use if the group members are not actively participating. In the Asbury and Carey (2005) project, it was expected that the children would benefit by having an exercise to lead into the discussion. This component of the study was informed by Dr. Asbury's experience as a former elementary school teacher. The drawing activity was appealing to the children and helped them to sit still during the discussion. This activity got them thinking about dreams and concerns, so that they could share information about factors that may stand between them and their goals.

In another example, a movie of activities important to the Hawaiian culture was shown before each focus group session in a study of wellness with Hawaiian elders (Odell, 2008). From her many years of experience as a nurse practitioner and having lived in Hawaii for many years, Odell (Chapter 2) had some understanding of the culture and of her limited insider status. The activities of fishing, surfing, and doing the hula were selected by Odell and local Hawaiian advisors as being central to the Hawaiian culture. The videotaping of the elders as they watched the film shows them really engaged—laughing with the funny sections, swaying to the music, and even talking to the person in the film. The focus group discussions that followed the showing of the film referred back to the film on several occasions.

Probing

Analysis begins during a session as the facilitator understands the comments and stories and follows up to clarify and to elicit further comments. The follow up, or probes, is essential to obtain data that are the most meaningful. It is important to note nonverbal information in order to understand responses and know when to probe. The facilitator observes any inconsistency between verbal and nonverbal responses, as well as changes in participants' comments during a session. Probes are used to explore inconsistencies—gently. The facilitator needs to understand the information well enough to follow the discussion and know when and how to probe. Generally, the facilitator cannot return to the group later to clarify comments. The facilitator has to exercise judgment in deciding when not to probe if the level of distress seems high or likely to escalate, or if the participant seems reluctant to further share.

Example 4: Probing

Facilitator: What do you do when you're in a situation like you talked about with peer pressure? What do you think about, what do you feel, what do you say?

Bonnie: I just tell them, No, back off, because I don't want my life to end up that way.

Facilitator: Do you just tell them "No," and you're real firm about it or what?

Bonnie: Yeah, I'd be real firm. I'd tell them that I don't want to be that way.

[The facilitator chose to not probe further here. The child's nonverbal behavior indicated that she did not intend to elaborate. With some participants, particularly children, the moderator must be careful not to be too forceful or to challenge when probing, or the children will be reluctant to speak.]

Facilitator: Is it hard to stay away?

Brad: I would tell them that I don't want to do it. I would feel like, uneasy. When I feel uneasy, like something in my stomach, I just try to get out of it the best way I can. But it's very hard, you know, to... because you think these people are your friends, and like... it's hard.

[Here, again, the moderator chose not to probe; did not ask how Brad got out of the trouble, because the point of the study was more about what coping strategies the children had to rely on when such situations arose.]

Facilitator: So how do you decide? How do you decide what to do?

Caren: Just stay away from them for a while.

Facilitator: Sometimes you avoid them...

[Here the facilitator trailed off, encouraging Caren to say more, but she did not.]

Facilitator: Anybody else have a different sort of strategy?

Jose: Get them in trouble.

Facilitator: So you tell someone else so that they can deal with the situation?

Bonnie: You gotta get people out of it. Sometimes they want to go in that direction, but you gotta actually get people out of it. Tell their parents or tell another person, like a guidance counselor, but sometimes people can't get them out of it because it's so serious.

Facilitator: So you're saying that sometimes telling an adult can be a good thing?

Bonnie: Yeah. Sometimes telling an adult won't get them in trouble. It can help them.

In this example, the facilitator is using follow-up questions to get a better understanding of what the children mean (*"Is it hard to stay?"*) and is exploring the depth of what they mean. Brad responded with comments on how he would feel—*"uneasy, like something in my stomach"*—and why it would be hard—*"these people are your friends."* The dialogue includes examples of not probing when it was deemed inappropriate.

Last Question

It can be very useful for facilitators to ask a "last question" that often elicits the most important data, because members are engaged in the topic and rapport has been established. A common phrasing is "If you could tell the people in charge just one thing, what would it be?" The facilitator can ask each member in turn to reply. In addition, leaving the tape recorder on as members leave the room usually collects very rich data; after having been involved in discussion, participants usually make thoughtful comments.

Example 5: Last Question

Facilitator: If you were in charge for a day, what programs would you create to help kids stay out of trouble and achieve their goals?

Jose: Help with schoolwork.

Brad: Have rec centers with sports teams and coaches.

Bonnie: A big park like Sea World.

Ian: More adults to watch kids after school.

Michael: More role models.

Caren: Trips to fun places.

Sasha: Someone here to talk to.

Facilitator Style and Session Structure

Focus groups are planned to be informal discussions, some more formal and structured than others, depending on the purpose. The decision to go with the flow or adhere more narrowly to the planned guideline questions will depend on the purpose and what the sponsoring organization requires, as well as the group's responses. If the topic is fairly well defined and a more narrow scope is planned, the structure may be more defined. If the group discussion leads in a direction not anticipated and the data seem important, the facilitator may choose to let the discussion continue in the new direction. Being flexible can enhance the collection of new and unanticipated information.

The facilitator may be someone known to the group members, such as a community service provider or health care provider. The group facilitator needs to keep in mind that the purpose of the session is data collection, not remedying problems or giving advice. Some group members may find it difficult to set aside the notion of the facilitator as anyone other than an expert; in such situations, another person will need to lead the sessions.

After the Session

For sensitive topics or when the session has covered emotionally charged topics, we recommend that the facilitator talk with the group members after the session—a type of debriefing focusing on the session itself and how the members are feeling (Tolich, 2009). Referrals for follow-up services can be made as needed.

Another type of debriefing can be done by the facilitator and the co-facilitator immediately after the session; they can leave the tape recorder turned on while they are discussing the session rather than initially taking notes. This type of unstructured review of the session can provide very valuable insights that will not be accessible in twenty-four hours; the richness of the details cannot be recalled as vividly as they can be immediately after the session. This discussion captures the facilitator's and co-facilitator's immediate recollection of the group members' response to the guideline questions, the type of interaction, the key points, the presence of a dominant or very talkative member and its effect, inconsistencies in comments, and what led to changes in members' comments.

Depending on the topic, study purpose, and the preference of the facilitator and co-facilitator, this debriefing could be extensive. The information can be reviewed to plan for refinement of the study process before the next session, and later it can be typed up into field notes.

Rigor

Considering rigor only at the end of the study will not be helpful in producing optimally useful results. A study's trustworthiness and utility, although often critiqued by others at the conclusion of the study, are more appropriately addressed through strategies employed during the study. Rigor has been described as involving credibility, transferability, dependability, and confirmability (Guba and Lincoln, 1989). Listening to the audiotape or watching the video recording and reviewing field notes as soon as possible will help to ensure appropriateness of the data.

Planning for ensuring rigor includes employing an audit trail, member checks of data, adequate categorization in analysis, peer debriefing with colleagues, and negative case analysis (Morse et al., 2002). An audit trail includes decisions and their rationale for each step in the study—raw data, field notes, data summaries, theoretical notes, and analysis. The audit trail helps to assist the reader in evaluating the soundness of the study. Member checks are done in the session as the facilitator checks with the participants that he or she has captured the main ideas. Peer debriefing with colleagues is an ongoing process to check that the process and insights are grounded in the data—both verbal and nonverbal.

Ethics

A researcher's primary ethical obligation is to the people whose lives are involved in the studies. There is a need to recognize the participants' perspectives of risks and benefits to them, to their communities, and to science. Issues include the consent process, confidentiality, required reporting, research team discomfort, online sessions, publishing, participants with diminished capacity, and ethics review board approval.

Informed consent is a process, not only a signed document. Agreement to participate is an ongoing process in research, not a one-time signature on a form. As we have described previously, the signing of a form may occur before the day of the session or just before beginning of the session. The reading level should generally not be beyond fifth grade, and, when appropriate, the form should describe possible future uses of data, such as secondary research. Participation in a session sometimes functions as having given consent, but this is not always appropriate. Oral consent may be appropriate for illiterate participants and is permitted in some situations.

Informed consent must be tailored to the specific population in terms of language as well as capabilities. Informed consent cannot be obtained from children; rather formal consent must be obtained from parents or guardians, and assent (agreement) from children. The age of consent/assent varies among localities. (A later chapter discusses the attention needed for special populations.)

Confidentiality presents unique ethical challenges in the context of a focus group; although researchers can protect the confidentiality of the data, they cannot guarantee that the group members will not relate to others what is said in the sessions. Also, members may divulge more information than they intended, especially on an emotional topic. This possibility of disclosing more than intended during the session also raises an issue of informed consent, because it is possible that a member may not have originally consented to such a disclosure. Such issues should be considered when planning the guideline questions, as well as training the group facilitator.

Required reporting—for example, of suspected child abuse or criminal behavior—needs to be made clear to group members if the topic could involve such information. Members need to understand the consequences of disclosing such information.

Monitoring the level of discomfort, especially related to sensitive topics, and having ready referral to support services should be part of planning. Debriefing participants regarding their level of comfort after the session is recommended (Tolich, 2009).

Listening to and analyzing data on very sensitive topics can lead to distress for the researchers (Carey and Swanson, 2003). Planning should include monitoring the discomfort of members of the research team and establishing a process for debriefing with professional support if needed.

Issues of confidentiality and expected privacy levels also require a level of knowledge of the effect of the medium used. For example, Stewart and Williams (2005) point out that when conducting online focus groups, some community members may divulge more information than in a traditional setting because of the "perceived anonymity, reduced social cues," and recognition of the time-space distance (p. 399). Cyber-rights groups' publications and relevant laws can guide ethical considerations concerning privacy and confidentiality in online research. Stewart and Williams point out the unique issues in online research involving identity theft, hacking, and data harvesting.

Protecting participants' identities in publishing and presenting findings can be a challenge. Using pseudonyms is one approach, but this is not always useful when a participant has a unique set of characteristics that could be used to identify him or her. It is possible to give participants the choice of being identified, or a composite character may be presented.

Approval is needed before data can be collected for research. Obtaining ethics review boards' approval or other needed approval has been a challenge for many types of qualitative research studies. This situation may be due in part to the boards' unfamiliarity with qualitative methods and the discomfort with the somewhat unstructured process of such studies.

The group interaction component is an additional challenge for obtaining research approval. Some ethic boards have community advisory groups who review proposals and identify issues of informed consent and feasibility. This type of review can foster understanding of the cultural and social context in the research process. Each organization or university will have its own approval forms and requirements that, although similar across organization, will differ somewhat.

Summary

The importance of planning is reflected in the length of this chapter, the longest in this book. Guided in planning by understanding a psychosocial theoretical foundation, the researcher can develop the research process and organize the logistics. Often adaptations or adjustments need to be made as information is developed and conditions change. Good-quality data—rich, detailed and representative comments—are crucial for the next step of analysis.

4. Implementing the Plan

This chapter provides guidance on conducting focus group sessions. Topics include group management skills, starting the session, session structure and facilitator role, probing, the role of the co-facilitator, ending the session, and handling problems.

Key Questions

4.1. What capabilities should a facilitator have?
4.2. What is the importance of the "ice breaker" question and the "last question"?

Group Management Skills

In group management, facilitator skills include monitoring participants' discomfort, guiding the discussion, and enhancing data quality. The facilitator must monitor the level of distress and refocus the group as needed and, in unusual cases, stop the session if a member becomes distressed. For some projects, facilitators will need professional education or clinical training in such fields as psychology, social work, nursing, counseling, and/or education. For sensitive topics or especially vulnerable populations, referral to competent support services should be readily available.

Interviewing skills are basic to enhancing data quality. In their introductory text, Rubin and Rubin (2005) provide sound advice for novice interviewers. Being able to listen to "what is behind the words" spoken—active listening—is a skill learned through practice and feedback (Kvale and Brinkmann, 2009).

Listening to a tape recording of a session, watching a videotape, or even just transcribing can help facilitators to develop listening skills. Some knowledge of the topic and of the participants is also needed to understand the comments well enough to guide the discussion and to ensure rich, detailed data. Hermanowicz (2002) provides a concise, witty guide for improving interviewing skills. He states that skilled interviewers have a quiet concern for the research participants and recognize that the interview proceeds through stages (revelations) and enacted rituals (introduction, explanation).

Managing a focus group is complicated, because the facilitator needs to encourage participation while maintaining a nonjudgmental style. The facilitator may restate that the purpose of the session is to encourage a variety of experiences, thereby conveying an expectation or norm for a range of comments. This setting is different from a classroom, where the instructor may be looking for a correct answer. For this reason, facilitators must self-monitor their nonverbal responses to comments—for example, nodding after a participant's comment may be perceived as agreement that the comment is correct.

Many groups include one or two members who tend to be dominant, and their frequent participation can limit the participation of other members. This situation can especially be a problem in a large group, such as 8 to 10 people, where there is limited time for each member to talk. So, in addition to thanking the talkative person and turning to the group to ask for other comments, the facilitator can physically indicate that other comments are welcome; for instance, if the talkative person has intentionally been seated next to the facilitator (as the result of observations made during the presession mingling), the facilitator can slightly turn her body away from the talkative person to face the others, thereby nonverbally reinforcing the norm of other contributions. Of course, this needs to be done tactfully, so as not to offend the talkative person.

Remember not to be too brief with a chatty member, or the rest of the group will also feel chastened and then be more reticent to speak. Recognizing the talkative person for her or his contribution will avoid offense. To help a reticent participant, we have found a simple approach to be effective: if this person has intentionally been seated directly across from the facilitator, the facilitator can encourage participation by making eye contact and restating the goal of listening to a range of experiences.

Starting the Session

After people have mingled around the food table, the facilitator begins the session with an introduction. This helps to establish rapport and trust.

Information about the project and the sponsoring organization, previously provided in the recruitment letter or phone call (see Chapter 3), is repeated, and any questions are answered. Agreement for recording will have been obtained earlier as part of the consent process, and this agreement is repeated now, before the video or audio taping is begun. Depending on the project's purpose, the group members are told that a range of experiences rather than agreement is the goal. As we have mentioned, this context encourages members to share comments that are not necessarily in agreement; they can feel comfortable in describing a range of opinions, because it has been made clear that there are no correct responses.

Two simple, helpful "rules" are these: no disparaging remarks about another member's comments, and only one person talks at a time, which prevents overlapping comments. Gentle reminders can keep interruptions to a minimum. The co-facilitator can draw a seating chart and record the order of the first few speakers in order to identify the speakers for the transcript. Cell phones and pagers should be turned off or, if members need to be reachable, turned to quiet mode.

Session Structure and Facilitator Role

In some studies, flip charts or other means of visual display have been used to record comments for the group to see. Although this process can be useful in some cases, it may give the impression of rewarding responses as correct and can dampen group interaction, making a broad range of experiences harder to obtain. The use of visual displays may be helpful when seeking agreement, but it is not usually helpful when the goal is exploring a range of experiences. If plans have been made for drawing a picture or showing a brief movie or a photo, this activity should follow the Introduction. Such data-elicitation techniques may be used in place of, or in addition to, guideline questions.

The study purpose, which may range from an exploratory study to model development, is the main factor in selecting how specific the guideline questions should be and the degree of flexibility in following them, with more open questions and flexibility used for more exploratory studies. The project may require that the session closely follow the guideline questions or explore in depth a narrow aspect of a particular topic. However, for an exploratory study, less direction from the facilitator, more flexibility in following the questions, and more openness of the questions can allow unanticipated data to be elicited. This openness will likely involve issues of importance to the members.

The facilitator "trains" the members for their role verbally by encouraging comments in their responses and nonverbally by making eye contact and paying close attention to comments, being careful to encourage comments without agreeing or approving. The facilitator may ask if anyone has had a different type of experience—thereby actively seeking a range and variation of comments. In eliciting and listening to comments, try to aim for four characteristics—depth, context, range, and specificity—recommended by Merton and colleagues (Merton, Kendall, and Fiske, 1990). Consider the causes and conditions that are part of the stories, especially for unusual cases. The facilitator needs to have ongoing engagement with the data to appreciate how the stories are related and how the synergy in the group is influencing the comments. Asking members to "think back" to the experience can help put them in the setting and bring out some of the richness of their experiences.

When incorrect information is stated, it is usually better to wait until the end of the session to provide correct information rather than intervening during the session. If the incorrectness is disturbing to the discussion, then the facilitator may provide enough information to help the discussion proceed. It is especially important to provide correct information when safety is involved, such as when incorrect comments involve the transmission of HIV. When the facilitator is known by the group members to have expert knowledge related to the study topic, it may be hard for her or him to stay in the role of researcher and not in the role of the expert to remedy problems. Professional and personal ethics may require following up on some problems and referring members to support services.

To concentrate on processing the comments, the facilitator needs to be able to judge if the general content of guideline questions and subquestions is being addressed. A group's discussion often does not follow the plan of guideline questions. Be flexible; generally, not every session needs to completely cover every question. For most studies, it is better to collect detailed, specific, personal information that is important to the members than to stay firmly with the planned questions.

The "ice breaker" question is an easy way to open the discussion. This gets members comfortable with speaking in the group. An ice breaker question used in the HIV study of the military by Carey and Smith (1994) was "How did you learn you had HIV?" This was easy to answer and helped to establish the common experience of the group members. In place of an ice breaker question, the Asbury and Carey (2005) study's facilitator had the children say their names as the tape recorder ran and then played back the tape. The children really enjoyed hearing their voices, which helped to get them comfortable with the recording and with the session.

Sometimes it is apparent when members are ready to move on to the next topic. At this point, it is often helpful to briefly summarize the main ideas (but not build a consensus). The natural flow of the discussion may not permit summarizing to be done comfortably, and it is not necessary for each question; an overall review of the main ideas at the end of the session is very helpful to enhance data quality. This "member checking" involves checking the main ideas for accuracy of understanding of the data collected. And leave time for the last question: "If you could tell the organization just one thing, what would it be?"

The facilitator monitors the group response to the guideline questions to see how well they are working, if they need to be refined, and if participants are engaged. Some researchers believe that it is important to keep the guideline questions unchanged for each session. Keeping the guideline questions unchanged could be required by the sponsor of the research. However, if the group is not responding, or if the group continues to take the discussion in different directions, often it is more appropriate to use the information from one group session to refine the questions for the next session.

Many topics in focus group studies will not lead to any stress or embarrassment, but some could. However, it has not been our experience, or the experience of our colleagues. The facilitator monitors stress levels and intercedes to guide the discussion in a safe direction; in extreme and very unusual cases the session may be stopped and referral services arranged. When one is facilitating sessions on sensitive topics, it can be helpful to allow members to describe a "friend's" experience. The researcher may suspect that the "friend's" story is actually the member's experience but that the member chooses to tell the story in another's voice. Such detachment may arise from a member's concern that the group will think poorly of him or her. The facilitator will judge how much to probe and how much to accept without inquiring further into the details.

Probing

A preliminary type of analysis begins while the researcher is conducting the sessions and processing the data in order to understand the data. Knowing when and how to follow up, or probe, is the most important aspect of guiding the session to elicit good-quality data. *Probing* refers to seeking further information, more details based on personal experience. Lack of agreement between verbal and nonverbal communications and inconsistent comments can be bases for probing. Personal and specific details improve the credibility and general quality of the data. The facilitator should consider the following questions in deciding when to probe: Is this a plausible story? Is it logically consistent? Do the nonverbal aspects match the verbal ones? When a member provides a general comment, the facilitator follows up with a request for more details and processes the comments in relation to his or her knowledge of the population and the topic.

Co-Facilitator

The co-facilitator usually sits in back or to the side of the group, or may sit next to the facilitator if equal group leadership is planned. He or she needs to be able to take notes and easily detect nonverbal expressions—including facial expressions, gestures, body position, and movements of hands, feet, head—and verbal expressions, including pace of speech, pitch, and intensity. This person also tends to the "host" concerns—food, late members, phone availability, and bathrooms.

Ending the Session

Researchers may keep the tape recorder turned on after the discussion has ended and members are leaving. The comments made as members are heading out the door may be the most useful. As the session is ending, the facilitator states again that the members can contact her or him if they have questions and again provides the contact information. If members seem upset, the facilitator and/or the co-facilitator will debrief them and provide referral information as needed. Then the facilitator and co-facilitator debrief each other. Check immediately to see that the tape recorder captured the data. If not, debrief on tape immediately.

A demographic questionnaire may be used to help describe the participants. Generally, it is better to have members answer the questionnaire at the end of the session so that it will not affect their contributions during the discussion.

Problems

Planning cannot prevent all problems. These are some of the more common issues: few people come ("no shows"), the discussion involves a "bandwagon" effect (apparent exaggeration), and/or the discussion flows in a direction not useful to the research.

If only one or two people come to a session, the researcher could consider this an interview, which, although not what was planned, could provide useful information. Try to learn why the other members, who had agreed to come, did not come, contacting them if possible. It may be that transportation is more difficult than anticipated or the physical setting is not comfortable—for example, a hospital may remind people of the death of a loved one. Also, the recruitment and reminder protocol could be modified.

A concern noted in some literature is the "bandwagon," or "group think," effect, which refers to the phenomenon of participants being carried along by the group interaction and agreeing with the overall discussion (Carey and Smith, 1994). This phenomenon usually involves negative comments but not positive comments. It is usually apparent when this problem is occurring, and it is regarded as a challenge for the facilitator to explore. Merton and colleagues' (Merton, Kendall, and Fiske, 1990) advice to explore depth and specific details can help to address this. It is important not to directly challenge the group members when one is asking for more information.

The issue of exaggeration is seldom mentioned in the literature as a concern, and in our experience and that of several of our colleagues, exaggeration does not occur often and can be fairly easy to recognize when it does occur. An example of exaggeration was noted in a focus group session of senior citizens held at a residential center (Carey, 1990). These members were familiar with one another and were likely to have future interaction. The topic of the focus group was health status after ambulatory surgery, and the purpose of the focus group was to understand experiences in order to develop a questionnaire to be mailed to elderly patients. One member described an experience that was medically implausible as well as inconsistent with the group discussion. The other group members gently but firmly questioned the speaker, who then revised his comments. If the group members had not questioned the speaker, the facilitator could have done so. Modification of the guideline questions may help to guide the responses. Probing needs to be done very tactfully, so as not to challenge but to explore the details.

Another example of exaggeration is described by Hollander (2004) in a session with young males discussing their experience of violent behavior. Hollander suggests that the apparent conformity to stereotypical male role of boldness and fighting ability, especially given the familiarity of members within the group, likely led to data that were not an adequate reflection of the members' experiences. The gradual escalation of the degree of violence described in the discussion was an indicator of bandwagon, or groupthink, effect. Even with excellent facilitator skills, one can find it difficult to counter this problem in some sessions. The poor quality of data will limit its usefulness. Infrequently, the group format might not work well because of the bandwagon effect.

The third type of problem involves the discussion flowing in a direction not useful to the research; the group comments may build on one another, and comments may be unrelated to the study. In some cases this situation may reveal issues that were not anticipated but are of importance to the group. When the facilitator feels the direction of the discussion is not useful, whether to bring it back to the planned guideline questions or let the discussion flow is a judgment call to be made during the session. Factors to consider are the intensity of the comments, the consensus of the members, and the level of the details. In reviewing the recording after each session, the facilitator can explore how and why such direction occurred and if refining the protocol is warranted.

Rigor

Aspects of rigor in conducting sessions mostly involve the skills of the facilitator in helping the group to explore the topic. Knowing when and how to probe is essential for collecting good-quality data; attending to the nonverbal aspects and clarifying inconsistencies are skills that may need to be developed with experience.

Ethics

As we described in earlier chapters, confidentiality must be monitored on an ongoing basis. The facilitator needs to be aware of the participants' ability to control their comments and help them not to disclose more than they intend. This need to monitor internal confidentiality is discussed in the preceding chapter. Another concern relates to an instruction that is given in some group settings that is not appropriate for focus groups. The researcher cannot, and should not, promise that "what is said in the room stays in the room." The researcher does not have this control and should not promise this.

Summary

This chapter presents guidelines for conducting focus groups, with an emphasis on probing to obtain good-quality data. Also discussed are approaches to group management, considerations for maintaining structure and being flexible, and suggestions for dealing with some potential problems. The next chapter highlights special considerations for planning and conducting focus group sessions with special populations.

5. Special Populations

This chapter highlights the usefulness of focus groups with people whose experiences are not well understood or not detailed in previous studies. We include suggestions for soliciting the desired information.

Key Questions

5.1. What makes a group a "special population"?

5.2. How do you address special populations' needs in planning issues of group size, length of session, and the match of facilitator and members' important demographic variables?

5.3. How do you include members of the target population in all aspects of planning, implementing, and analyzing?

Definition

The Department of Health and Human Services, Office of Human Research Protections (*www.hhs.gov/ohrp/archive/irb/irb_chapter6.htm*), identifies groups whose welfare requires special consideration. These groups include those who are at greater than average risk for harm, given their circumstances or societal position. Such populations are referred to as "special" or "vulnerable" in the research literature. For our purposes in discussing the use of focus groups as a research approach, we specifically concentrate on using focus groups with children, minorities, elders, gay/lesbian/bisexual/ transgendered participants, and the cognitively or emotionally impaired. This emphasis is, in part, shaped by the nature of the research approach but also by the parameters of the published research. However, any group

Focus Group Research by Martha-Ann Carey and Jo-Ellen Asbury, 69–78 © 2012 Left Coast Press, Inc. All rights reserved.

falling within the scope of the description should be considered "special" by the research team, and extra precautions should be put in place. For example, recent studies have used the term "vulnerable" in reference to Holocaust survivors (Barel et al., 2010), those at greater risk of contracting HIV (Albarracin et al., 2008), African-American adolescents coping with parental breast cancer (Kissil et al., 2010), and those with intellectual disabilities (Morin et al., 2010).

Focus Groups with Children

It has been suggested that focus groups are particularly useful with children, because this approach facilitates a reduction in the power imbalance between the facilitator and the participants (Heary and Hennessy, 2002; Morgan et al., 2002). Hill (2006) notes that focus groups enable a true collaboration between the facilitator and child participants. Furthermore, focus groups promote children's active participation in the research process and thus improve the investigator's access to their worldview. Focus groups can empower the child participants (Horner, 2000) and place them in the role of expert (Heary and Hennessy, 2002). Darbyshire, MacDougall, and Schiller (2005) echo this sentiment by suggesting that focus groups enable one to do research "with" children rather than "on" them. However, given their developmental level and particular vulnerabilities, children in a focus group require attention in ways beyond what we have discussed so far.

Much of the research using focus groups with children targets specific populations who share a particular health issue (for example, Darbyshire et al., 2005; Fitzpatrick et al., 2009; Morgan et al., 2002), and those investigations have shown this methodological approach to be particularly useful with these groups. Sharing a particular health concern facilitated the connection among the children and helped to focus their contributions to the group discussion. However, the use of focus groups with children need not be limited to those with common health concerns. We conducted a community needs assessment study (Asbury and Carey, 2005) with healthy children and found that they were very able participants, when alternate activities were used to help focus their remarks.

Issues unique to the use of focus groups with children include: ages (and range of ages included), need for gender segregation, size of the group, whether or not friends should be included within the same group, setting, developing appropriate level of language for question wording, understanding children's responses, dealing with somewhat abstract concepts, and how long children can be expected to tolerate the focus group discussion. Published studies are not always in agreement regarding guidance offered on these issues.

Heary and Hennessy (2002) recommend not using focus groups with children under 6 years of age, because they do not have the language and social skills to be effective participants. Darbyshire and associates (2005), however, reported using focus groups with children as young as 4 years of age. Most suggest (for example, Hoppe et al., 1995; Kennedy et al., 2001) that the range of ages should be limited to a one- to two-year difference across group participants.

Depending on the age of the children, and the topic, groups may need to be gender segregated. Morgan and colleagues (2002) used mixed gender groups for children 10 years old and under, but used gender-segregated groups for 11-year-olds. We have used mixed-gender groups with children and teens (Asbury and Carey, 2005) when topics did not involve particularly sensitive gender issues.

Guidance on the optimal size for focus groups with children is generally consistent with that for groups with adults. Recommendations regarding group size (Hoppe et al., 1995; Kennedy et al., 2001; Morgan et al., 2002; Nabors, Ramos, and Weist, 2001) range from 4 to 8 children per group. Although 6 to 10 is probably the optimum upper limit, we would not recommend a group smaller than 3 to 4 children. Too few and there may not be enough participants willing to speak out; too many and the investigator's ability to differentiate individual contributions during the group and in reviewing the audio tapes later is significantly hindered. Further, with too few children, it is difficult for them not to view the facilitator as an authority figure in charge of the group. Including children who already know one another and are comfortable discussing the subject matter of the focus group might ameliorate this effect.

In general, the literature suggests that children are more comfortable in focus groups with children whom they already know, and this has generally been our experience as well. However, Morgan and colleagues (2002) noted that pre-adolescent boys were reluctant to admit vulnerabilities regarding their asthma in front of their schoolmates, whereas boys of the same age in the same group who did not know any of the other participants were more open. Of course, we cannot know for certain how much of that observed difference was due to personality and not mere familiarity. Such reticence is something to watch for in groups where the children are already familiar with one another; use additional probes to better determine if previous familiarity is an issue.

As with adults, a setting familiar to the children is helpful. Familiarity allows children to feel comfortable and safe. We conducted focus groups at the location of an after-school homework assistance program. This was particularly helpful in reducing the "adult as authority" dynamic, because it allowed us to defer to the children for such basic things as the location of the light switch or directions to the restrooms.

Obviously, the questions asked of children in focus groups must be developmentally appropriate. In addition to getting feedback from those knowledgeable of the target age group(s), pretesting the questions with children who will not be participating in the groups is helpful.

The level of abstraction of the topic(s) that can be discussed is enhanced by having the children engage in various activities that help to focus their thoughts. For example, Nelson-Gardell (2001) used a worksheet with teenage girls that they could refer to during the discussion. Horstman and colleagues (2008), Driessnack (2006), and Kennedy and associates (2001) used drawings, as did we. In our study the children were asked to draw a picture about what they wanted their life to be like in the future. With this concrete goal in mind, they were then able to very adeptly discuss things that might interfere with reaching their goals. Because the purpose of our investigation was to assess the needs of the community in keeping their young people on a desirable life path, the drawings were invaluable.

The duration of individual focus group sessions needs to be developmentally appropriate as well. About 60 minutes has been suggested for pre-adolescent children (about 10–14 years) (Kennedy et al., 2001; Nabors et al., 2001), less (about 45 minutes) for younger children (Morgan et al., 2002), and longer (90 minutes) for teens (Nelson-Gardell, 2001). Keim and associates (1999) found that some third graders could not stay focused more than 30 minutes. These boundaries can be extended if participants are given concrete tasks to help to occupy their hands or help to focus their attention (Nelson-Gardell, 2001). (See above and our discussion on data elicitation in Chapter 3.) Our experiences with traditionally aged college students (late adolescents) suggest that, even with food, 90 minutes is about as much as they can tolerate.

Ethnic Minority and Cultural Groups

The significance of the history of minority groups in this country should not be overlooked in any research approach and certainly not in focus group studies. Scholars concerned about the cultural legitimacy of research (for example, Clark, 1972; Hughes and DuMont, 1993; Sue, 1983) have long suggested that our investigations need to try to understand the worldview of our participants and do research "with" them rather than "on" them. Hughes and DuMont (1993) note that focus groups are a particularly useful tool for achieving this objective. Vogt, King, and King (2004) also note the benefits of using focus groups to allow researchers to learn the meaning of constructs from the perspective of the population studied. They go on to note that this is important, because researchers may unconsciously interpret the experiences of other cultures through their own cultural lens, leading to ethnocentric assumptions and interpretations of behaviors and experiences. (See Hennink [2008] for a discussion on international focus groups.)

In addition to planning issues already discussed in Chapters 3 and 5, concerns unique to research with underrepresented groups include appropriate language or phrasing of the questions, which is important to the success of the research. As has already been suggested, soliciting feedback from those knowledgeable of the target population and/or piloting the questions with individuals who are members of the cultural group but who will not be participating in the focus group can be helpful.

Whether or not the members are willing to reveal information in the context of the focus group must also be considered. Again, extra steps may need to be taken to establish rapport and to help the members to feel comfortable discussing the topic(s) of interest. Depending on the topic, it may be particularly important to discuss group ground rules and issues of confidentiality. Finally, whether the facilitators are members of the same group as the group participants is also a consideration in planning.

Shrank and colleagues (2005), using ethnically segregated groups with same-race facilitators and co-facilitators, conducted focus groups with African-Americans and non-Hispanic Whites and found clear difference in some aspects of their preferences for palliative care. Gany and associates (2006), using focus groups segregated by immigrant versus non-immigrant status, identified factors that may explain the disproportionately higher cancer (lung, prostate, breast, and cervical) incidents and mortality rates among immigrant minority groups, compared to U.S.-born minority groups. Gany and colleagues (2006) also segregated their groups by gender, as might be expected, given the topic. However, Orel (2004) found that although age and sexual orientation were important variables to consider in recruiting, ethnicity was not. As we noted in Chapter 3, you must consider what matters and is relevant to the research focus as group members are recruited. Although under some circumstances participants might feel more comfortable in ethnically segregated groups, some life experiences transcend ethnicity or other demographic variables that might otherwise be paramount.

Lesbian/Gay/Bisexual/Transgender (LGBT) Groups

Allen (2006) used focus group with LGBT teens in order to "open a space for 'subversive' discussion" (p. 173) about their experiences. Allen found the focus group approach to be particularly useful in "destabilizing heterosexuality as normalized sexual identity" (p. 168). In the course of her discussions with the LGBT youth, Allen reported a number of ways in which the members of her groups demonstrated the heterosexual norm in society and the ways in which their experiences were not included. The members noted, for example, how much of sexual education in their school focused on reproduction and how not to get pregnant. This is not a concern for self-identified gay or lesbian youths, an insight that likely would have been overlooked with a different methodological approach.

Allen's (2006) study is also of interest in relation to the question of whether the facilitator needs to be a member of the target group. Allen was not a member of the target group but took steps (for instance, removing her wedding ring) to minimize her "outsiderness." Thus, this situation suggests that when one cannot achieve insider status, steps need to be taken to gain trust, establish a rapport, and minimize differences between the facilitator(s) and the members.

Orel (2004) studied gay/lesbian/bisexual seniors, a group that has garnered little attention yet is growing in number owing to longer life expectancies. In this case, focus groups were used as a precursor to instrument development. Given how little research attention has been devoted to this group, and how different from younger LGBTs their experiences and perspectives are likely to be, focus groups were used to explore their needs, concerns, and issues.

Elderly Participants

Of primary concern with elderly participants are issues related to the normal aging process, such as physical ability to access the selected setting, physical comfort, auditory acuity, and ability to articulate their thoughts. Planning should be structured accordingly. In some instances, the cognitive functioning of the elderly might need to be considered, although this should not be universally assumed to be a concern.

Similar to work discussed above with children, a number of studies bring seniors together to discuss particular health concerns. Ivanoff (2002) is one example of this, having found focus groups to be uniquely useful with elderly persons with age-related macular degeneration. Information resulting from Ivanoff's groups was intended to inform the development of a health education program.

Recent published articles include a number of examples of using focus groups to explore preferences in palliative care and quality-of-life issues. Interestingly enough, the questions of segregated versus nonsegregated groups again emerged. Bito and associates (2007) and Bullock and colleagues (2005) used ethnically segregated groups to explore end-of-life care issues. Leung and associates (2004) used segregated groups to explore quality-of-life issues. These studies relied on the guidance of previous research that suggested that there were issues unique to the respective cultural groups that indicated a culture-specific focus for their inquiries.

Persons with Cognitive or Emotional Disabilities

Sources point to focus groups as a useful approach with individuals with cognitive or emotional impairments, because these groups do not require a specific level of literacy, offer a more informal setting, and can help facilitate the contributions of those who might otherwise feel that they had little to contribute (Gibbs, Brown, and Muir, 2008). In many cases, focus groups are used with these groups (and/or their caretakers) to gain more in-depth information that could ultimately lead to improved services and access to services. Castellblach and Abrahamson (2003), Gibbs and associates (2008), and Stacciarini (2008) offer examples of focus group studies of this type.

Of primary concern in research involving individuals with psychiatric, cognitive, or developmental disorders is that their disorders may compromise their ability to understand the information presented and their ability to make a reasoned decision about participation (*www.hhs.gov/ohrp/archive/irb/irb_chapter6.htm#g5*). Fenton and colleagues (2009) offer an example of using multiple methods involving multiple constituent groups to explore the research questions. Focus groups were used to elicit the perceptions of mental health rehabilitation staff, whereas a photography project was used with people actually using the rehabilitation services.

Other Populations

We use this category to make the point that any group of people having had a unique experience that is not well understood by others may be classified as "vulnerable" and thus require special considerations as we design and plan our research studies. A complete list of those to whom this might apply to is certainly beyond the scope of this book and would likely be outdated before it went to press. Thus, the examples offered here are indeed only illustrations of the myriad of possibilities.

Pfefferbaum and colleagues (2008) used focus groups to explore the experiences of children displaced by Hurricane Katrina. These authors stress the significance of gaining full understanding of what the children experienced rather than relying on assumptions in trying to provide services. Dunlap and associates (2009) used focus groups to explore how drug users, also displaced by the hurricane, were able to find and access the networks needed to obtain drugs in their new location. As other catastrophic events occur, the unique experiences of groups such as the Hurricane Katrina survivors will need to be considered.

Rigor

With the groups discussed in this chapter there is often a greater need to watch for approval seeking between or among members. With children, this may be particularly necessary when the group comprises children who know one another (for example, Morgan et al., 2002). This is not to suggest, however, that this need is limited to children; any situation in which the members feel particularly unsure of their responses is likely to result in some form of self-censoring or conformity.

Also of particular importance with the groups discussed here is the need to sometimes include members of the target community in aspects of the data analysis. Such input may be necessary in being able to glean an adequate understanding of the members' contributions. Given the risk of cross-cultural misunderstanding, as discussed earlier, this inclusion may be of particular usefulness.

Ethics

Issues of informed consent are of particular importance with vulnerable populations. Whether those recruited are legally able to provide consent and are capable of understanding the focus and any risks of the research project must be considered. In work with minors, it is customary to obtain consent from their legal guardians but also to obtain the child's assent to participate in the focus group. For adults with cognitive or intellectual impairments or other forms of diminished capacity, in the consent process it is generally best to consult with a family member who is ultimately responsible for the potential member.

Working with vulnerable populations may require special justification. The aim of the research must be non-exploitative, with the research results benefitting the community in focus. The research should address the needs that the members themselves deem important or valuable, and the research should be related to the inherent characteristic that creates the vulnerability in the population.

Total confidentiality, especially with children, should not be promised, because a problem could arise when the facilitator is obligated to inform the parent or responsible party if a group member divulges dangerous or illegal behavior or plans. It is the responsibility of the research team to be aware of local protection laws and policies.

Summary

Taken together, the literature and experiences reviewed here suggest that with any unique, special, or vulnerable populations care must be taken in recruitment strategies to be certain that participants will be comfortable contributing within the context of the focus group setting. Whether this means segregating group members into certain demographic categories depends on the research focus.

Additional steps may also be necessary in establishing trust and an appropriate rapport with the participants. Whether it is important that the facilitator share the key characteristics, not only demographic characteristics, with the target group must be considered early in the planning stage. Trade-offs and practical constraints must be considered in deciding to use an experienced facilitator who does not share those key characteristics or training someone who does.

Given these groups' vulnerability, it may be particularly problematic if a member reveals something that he or she did not intend to. Thus, you must do your best to anticipate the eventuality and also to manage the group in a way as to minimize this occurrence.

In the next chapter we discuss strategies for analyzing the focus group data and how those approaches might vary with the research purpose.

6. Analysis

To help the researcher to develop a clear and convincing picture of findings, in this chapter, we address common issues, group context and interaction, analytic approaches, software, and rigor. An example of preliminary inductive analysis of a transcript and an audit trail is provided at the end of this chapter.

Key Questions

6.1. What are the common analysis methods used with focus group data? How are they selected?

6.2. Why is counting generally inappropriate?

Common Issues

The purpose of analysis is to understand the experiences of the participants and to communicate the findings so that they may be readily used. Analysis is often regarded as the most important component of focus group studies, because it has a direct impact on the usefulness of the findings. However, analysis of focus group data is the least well established. Analysis begins during the group session as the facilitator processes the comments, follows up to clarify or further explore them, and summarizes main ideas for the group to review. Sometimes analysis is assumed to be easy; however, depending on the study's purpose, analysis can be detailed and labor intensive.

Study findings can be data rich and analysis poor; that is, they are under-analyzed relative to the study's purpose. There are few, if any, agreed-on

Focus Group Research by Martha-Ann Carey and Jo-Ellen Asbury, 79–94 © 2012 Left Coast Press, Inc. All rights reserved.

rules for qualitative analysis. Because each study is unique, guidelines need to be used with creativity and judgment (Patton, 2002). Charmaz (2006) recommends "imaginatively engaging" with the data and then solidly grounding the interpretation directly in the data. This recommendation encourages the researcher to explore the possibilities that are not immediately obvious, thereby examining patterns that at first are not apparent. This approach can produce new and important theoretical development.

The selection of analytic method varies with the study's purpose, which was chosen in the planning stage, and the researcher's understanding of the data within a psychosocial context. Boundaries of some of the qualitative research methods are blurred (Starks and Trinidad, 2010), as described later in this chapter. Approaches range from staying quite close to the data and identifying broad themes to developing explanatory theory through interpretation and synthesis. Most qualitative methods used with focus groups studies have several components in common: identification of a topic, development of a sampling plan, collection of data, inductive coding and further iterative grouping of concepts, prioritizing of key ideas, and the use of the researcher as instrument in data collection and analysis. Generally, multiple readings of transcripts are done to ensure that codes and themes are well grounded in the data.

Similar to other qualitative data-collection techniques, saturation is considered reached when themes are completely developed and additional data provide no new information. Studies with a briefer descriptive purpose may not intend to reach saturation; rather, plans will include data collection that is adequate for the purpose. For example, in the Carey and Smith (1992) study with active duty U.S. military we explored the experience of having a diagnosis of HIV and participating in an intensive biopsychosocial study. We questioned if the standard psychosocial instruments and the heavy response burden might compromise the quality of the data. The research protocol was modified based in large part on the information from the focus groups. No intensive data analysis was performed; rather, a summary of experiences was useful. The purpose (goal), process (sampling and analysis), and product (new knowledge of the research protocol experience) were methodologically coherent, and the inquiry was very useful to this large, federally funded study.

Coding organizes the data to prepare for further analysis and interpretation. This process organizes the text and other data, such as nonverbal data and notes, into units of analysis that are analyzed for emergent themes (Lofland and Lofland, 1995). This type of analysis is called *inductive analysis*, which refers to the process of reasoning from the level of specific units to broader concepts. Some terms in qualitative inquiry are defined in various ways; in this book we follow Morse (2008) in defining *category* as a collection of data that has been coded into similar hunks, and further examination determines the major commonalities. Next, relationships between categories are examined to identify *themes*, which are broader, overarching cognitive units of meaning. There needs to be a clear description of the steps taken in the process of developing findings. Ideally, this description includes raw data, field notes, data summaries, theoretical notes, and synthesis including codes, themes, definitions, relationships, category decisions, and their rationale.

The unit of analysis may vary with different approaches, ranging from coding line by line to coding large hunks of text. Line-by-line coding is useful for in-depth studies with the goal of developing theory. However, this approach could lose the group context, because line-by-line coding fractures data into bits, and it can be more difficult to interpret within the group influence. In more descriptive studies, coding larger units may be appropriate. Understanding the comments and stories, not the group and not the individual, is the focus of analysis. Characteristics of the group interactions, sequence of statements, emotional expressions, and nonverbal gestures are used to explore the meanings behind the words.

Because the rich details of the session are not captured in most audio recordings and notes, the facilitator should do a preliminary analysis as soon as possible after a session and before the next session. This analysis would not involve using transcripts but rather a thorough review of notes and listening to the tapes or watching the video. You will be able to recall much less of the rich details twenty-four hours later. When reading transcripts or listening to tapes, listen for what is not said but you might expect to hear. Consider why what you expected was not discussed. What did you expect, and why? You might consider revising the guideline questions for the next session.

There are a few other suggestions that apply to most analysis. To assist with analysis, use the translator or a person who shares the same culture or ethnicity. Insight from one who knows the nuances of the local culture can be valuable. Beware of over-generalizing from quotes. Although a quote can encapsulate and convey the essence of a theme, a quote does not necessarily represent anyone's experience.

Group Context and Interaction

There is increasing attention to the need to incorporate the group context in understanding and analyzing focus group data (Duggleby, 2005; Kidd and Parshall, 2000; Morrison-Beedy, Cote-Arsenault, and Feinstein, 2001).

As part of any group setting, group dynamics affect the information collected. An analysis of group interaction could be the purpose of a study; however, this type of study generally would not be considered a focus group research project. It is more appropriate to consider group interaction data as an essential part of the context needed to understand and interpret the comments. In contrast to Morgan (2010) and Farnsworth and Boon (2010), we do not separate the group interaction data from what is said, because we see interaction as an integral part of understanding the data. It is important not to privilege one component (words alone) over the other (dynamics) (Halkier, 2010).

For some sessions, the group interaction will have little or no effect on the data; the synergy of the group will be useful mainly in enhancing participation. The main areas where context needs to be considered in interpretation are studies involving sensitive topics, special (vulnerable) populations, status differential among members in a session, members having little experience with being in a group, and the possibility of potentially adverse consequences of participation, especially, as we have mentioned, with the expectation of continued contact among participants.

The facilitator will need knowledge of the topic and the population to be able to interpret the data. Although there are no formal rules, the following suggestions can help you explore the data.

- Look for consistency and variation within a member.
- Listen for the rationale used to explain a belief/opinion and for what swayed a member to change his or her opinion. Sources of information include body language, tone, gestures, and other nonverbal communication, such as pauses.
- Note spontaneous responses as compared with responses to questions or follow-up probes.
- Note how a comment was made—concretely with details, vaguely or via third-person comments, in a raised voice, or defensively. It may be that spontaneous comments are associated with more vivid experiences.
- Note the intensity of opinions expressed.

Do not count! Merely counting the frequency of responses on a given topic will not only generally be inappropriate; it could also lead to misinterpretation (Carey, 1995). A group session has a chemistry and a dynamic that are more than the sum of its members' comments. Because data are elicited in response mostly to members' comments and to a lesser degree to the facilitator's questions and probes, the data are very much a function of each group. In a different mix of members, the data collected could, and likely would, be at least somewhat different, because comments are made in response to other comments. Therefore, most of the specific data are not directly comparable across groups, and detailed comparisons across sessions are generally not appropriate.

It is better to examine broad themes. When planning for groups to be segmented, such as by demographics, plan for two or more groups per segmented cell. For example, if gender and age are two dimensions that would likely affect group discussions and therefore will be used in segmenting groups, plan for two groups of older men, two groups of younger men, and so on. In that way, the unique group dynamics can be explored.

Analytic Approaches

The mostly commonly used methods in published studies of focus group research are based on inductive reasoning. These include thematic analysis, discourse analysis, content analysis, narrative analysis, and grounded theory, and there are many variations of each of these. Although possible to use with focus group data, phenomenology is not well suited, because this approach involves quite extensive data collection from a small number of people. The following paragraphs briefly define each of the common analytic approaches, describe how they are useful to focus group studies, and provide an example and references.

Thematic analysis is widely used to broadly identify, analyze, and describe patterns or themes. It can also be used in additional interpretation. This approach can be applied within many qualitative analyses. The usual steps, similar to most qualitative methods, include immersion in the data, development of codes, coding of data that are merged with field notes, identification of themes, and review for refinement. This approach does not allow you to explore with a sophisticated and deep analysis for model development. Especially because thematic analysis is so flexible, it is important to provide a detailed description of the process and assumptions. Braun and Clarke (2006) have published a recommended checklist to ensure rigor. Baldry, Green, and Thorpe (2006) examined the views and experiences of Aboriginal people living in Sydney, Australia. In addition to supporting findings from previous work, thematic analyses revealed the exceptional helpfulness of the liaison officers and the difficulty the Aboriginals had in accessing services. Focus groups were an exceptionally good method of working with this minority population, because the group sessions matched their cultural traditions.

Discourse analysis is an umbrella term encompassing various approaches that examine the function of language in how people construct their worlds. Although this approach is used less commonly with focus groups, it can provide important information. Language is examined as a social process, reflecting the production and interpretation of meanings; going beyond only representing reality, language constructs meaning (Fairclough, 1993). Using focus groups to collect data and using discourse analysis to analyze the data, Guise, McKinlay, and Widdicombe (2010) studied the effect of a stroke on the patient's identity. By exploring how language is used in social interactions, they found that stroke victims minimized their negative descriptions of the impact of their disabilities, but not so much as to be seen by their caregivers as inappropriately positive. The interactions in the focus groups assisted in collecting the depth of the data.

Content analysis has been broadly defined as using subjective interpretation and a systematic classification of coding and identifying patterns (Hsieh and Shannon, 2005). Content analysis can be used with quantitative or qualitative data, and it can be used inductively or deductively (Elo and Kyngas, 2007). One can start without a framework to explore concept development, or begin with a framework to validate or extend a theory. Similar to most qualitative methods, content analysis examines latent content to study underlying meanings (Morse and Field, 1995). There is some similarity between content analysis and thematic analysis. Patton (2002) describes the general focus of content analysis as looking for patterns (for example, most students are anxious at exam time) and thematic analysis as exploring more categorical concepts (fear is noted across many settings). Strickland, Walsh, and Cooper (2006) sought the parents' and elders' perspectives on resources needed to address the high rate of suicide in a Pacific Northwest American Indian tribe. Using content analysis to examine focus group data, the researchers identified the stressors and risk factors and the need to hold onto cultural values, keep family together, and obtain an education and a job. The concept of family was found to be understood differently than it is in mainstream America, and suicide prevention programs need to be aimed at strengthening the family.

Narrative analysis examines the stories people tell of their lives and experiences, with the goal of understanding social life and social practices. Actions are understood as a meaningful part of a story. Data are not fractured; rather, the focus is on long segments of talk organized around time, past and future events, and relationships with others (Reissman, 1993). Narratives exist in many layers and reflect belief systems. The narratives generally have a plot that includes a beginning, middle, and end (Creswell, 2008). Using cardiovascular patients' stories, Andreas and associates (2010) describe how patients use stories to provide coherence to their experiences, as contrasted with medical personnel's reliance on biomedical information.

Grounded theory is probably the most widely used method in qualitative research. It was developed in the 1960s and has evolved into several approaches (Charmaz, 2006; Corbin and Strauss, 2008; Glaser, 1995). The common elements include engaging simultaneously with data and performing analysis, developing codes and then categories rising from descriptive level to conceptual level, sampling purposefully based on the topic, memo writing, and often moving to advancing theory. Deitrick and colleagues (2010) used a grounded approach to analyze focus group data for a study of the usefulness of *promotoras* (local, ethnically similar women) for providing education in self-management of diabetes. The Spanish-speaking patients reported a high level of satisfaction and especially appreciated having the *promotoras* teach in their native language. Patients also reported increased self-esteem and empowerment, which are important to improved clinical outcomes and other quality of life outcomes.

Software

Software can be a helpful tool to organize the large amounts of data that are often involved in a project. A careful researcher will avoid premature labeling of categories, as occasionally is a criticism with software. It does take time to master a software programs in order for it to be a helpful tool and not a nuisance. Newer programs are capable of using videotapes, and some have voice recognition capability to provide rapid transcripts. Software programs such as Leximancer (Cretchley et al., 2010) promise to describe group dynamics beyond what researchers can do with other software. Software's automatic coding and grouping will likely be met with skepticism by some researchers who value the in-depth involvement of the researcher in understanding the text. It will be interesting to keep an open mind and see what enhancements are helpful as technology continues to advance.

Rigor

The goal of rigor does not vary with different research purposes; rather, the level of detail in analysis varies. For readers to evaluate the worth of the study findings, they need to know not only what was found but also how it was found. Adequate details need to be provided of the process of moving from raw data to codes, to categories, and to themes, depending on the purpose of the study. Verification strategies are used to enhance reliability and validity of the research process, not used merely at the conclusion to examine findings (Morse et al., 2002). These strategies include methodological coherence, concurrent data collection and analysis, and theory development as appropriate to the research purpose. Similar to analysis of data gathered with other qualitative techniques, documentation of the process and procedures will help readers to evaluate the quality and usefulness of the findings.

Field notes of insights and interpretation, including notes from the facilitator and co-facilitator debriefing after each session, are important in understanding the data. It is also helpful to include a person similar to the participants to help to understand the nuances. In our example of the focus groups with children (Asbury and Carey, 2005), it was not possible to have a same-age student help—the maturity level was not appropriate. However, during the sessions, the facilitator repeated the main ideas to check that she had heard correctly and to check that her interpretations were appropriate. The students were not shy about correcting her; they seemed to enjoy this process.

Ethics

There are a few ethical concerns related to analysis. These issues include secure data storage and timely deletion of data. (Data-security issues are not unique to focus group projects.)

Sample Analysis

The following example of an analysis and audit trail (Box 6.1) has been adapted from several of our experiences. This example represents some aspects of conducting and analyzing focus groups. The transcript begins after the session introduction and the children have agreed to have the tape recorder turned on. (Their parents provided consent earlier.) This is the first session, when the researcher is trying out the guideline questions and becoming familiar with the experiences of the children. Later sessions would more specifically target the children's needs in relation to their perception of available resources, which was the study's purpose.

We have coded only broad segments of text for this phase of the study. In the next phase, we would use the emerging categories and the potential theme to focus the data collection (theoretical sampling) and fully develop a model. Our example here uses inductive analysis, a process that is common to most qualitative methods and that proceeds from specific data to more general concepts (Patton, 2002). As you will see, the transcript is coded, the codes are then grouped into preliminary categories, and the beginning of a theme is noted. Codes are in **bold** and **underlined**.

This example is mostly at the descriptive level, with the plan to move to the conceptual level as categories are more fully developed and the themes clearly emerge. The findings would then be compared with the existing literature on risk and protective factors (Hawkins, Catalano, and Miller, 1992; Kumpfer and Alvarado, 2003). The audit trail would be added to as the work progresses.

Box 6.1

Facilitator: When people say a kid is a bad kid, what do they mean? Think about the people you know, kids your age. What kinds of trouble do kids your age get into?

    <No response. Facilitator asks a more concrete question.>

Facilitator: Do you know people about your age who have tried alcohol? Cigarettes?

Brad: My cousin, she's 13.   **Family problem**

Bonnie: My parents.

Facilitator: <laughs> But they're not people your age.

    <Some group members laugh together. Joking helps group members feel at ease.>

Facilitator: What about people roughly your age, people you know? Have any of your friends ever tried alcohol?

    <Getting more specific details.>

Ian: Yes.

Caren: Someone brought some to school.   **Acquaintance problem**

Facilitator: Somebody brought some to school? Somebody who's about your age?

    <Gets more details.>

Caren: Yes. And he got caught and suspended.

Facilitator: That's somebody who is about your age?

    <Gets details without getting too specific with the child.>

Caren: Yes and he drinks, smokes, and steals.

Facilitator: Did he just do it once or is it often?

Caren: More than once.

Facilitator: And he gets caught, and he goes to jail?

    <Caren nods but shrinks back and seems reluctant to continue. Facilitator does not probe.>

Facilitator: Caren mentioned a person who was stealing. Do you know people who are stealing?

    <Many voices...>

Bonnie: A kid up our street... he took $10 from a woman.

        Neighborhood problem

Facilitator: Do you know other people who have been arrested?

    <Asking for more details of other children's experiences.>

Ian: One time, not too long ago, during the summer, I was at the park over here. You could say it was being at the wrong place at the wrong time.

Facilitator: And so what happened?

Ian: This boy, he was throwing rocks at cars and he happened to hit a policeman's car. So we all ran.

Michael: Why did you run if you didn't do anything?

Ian: I was just scared. The car backed up... we thought "here it comes," so we all just started running. Two people ran up the alley. And my friend, he almost got caught. I was up the street, and I coulda went home but I went back to go check on him. He had gotten away and headed for home and I went to check on the other ones, and when I was leaving, when I turned the corner, the police officer was coming toward me. **Responsibility for friends**

Facilitator: So tell me, do you know any kids your age who have smoked marijuana or have done other kinds of drugs?

<Asking for more details.>

Michael: Yep, my brother. **Family problem**

Facilitator: Other kids your age?

<Indistinct murmuring…>

Facilitator: What about the rest of you? People you go to school with? Kids your age?

Sasha: My friend. She's 11, and her sister do it too and she's 10. **Friend problem**

Facilitator: Let me ask you a question. A lot of you have talked about knowing people who do some of these kinds of things, and you've implied that you don't. So what is the difference between you and them? How come you are able to NOT do those things when some other kids do?

Caren: I did one thing… kinda like smoking, but I don't want to say because people here go to my school. **Moral awareness**

<Self-censoring. Facilitator chose not to probe.>

Bonnie: I did some things… but… I learned my lesson.

Facilitator: Well tell me about that… tell me in as much detail as you are comfortable with. Tell me what made you decide, no, this isn't the path for me.

<Probes for reasons behind behavior.>

Bonnie: At first I did it and I wanted to… and then when we got out of the trouble, my friends wanted to do it again, but I just went home because they were going to steal some outfits. And a couple of them, they got caught. **Friends problem/Peer pressure/Moral awareness**

Facilitator: So that made the difference for you, you just decided you did not want to get caught?

Bonnie: Yeah. People want to try things, but when you hear in the news that people are getting drunk and in car accidents, it just changes your whole concept of the thing. People have nasty thoughts sometimes and when they are mad they want to go off and do bad things. But, when I'm mad, I just go to my room. **Moral awareness/Avoidance**

Michael: We have a lot of pressure from friends. **Peer pressure**

Facilitator: So how do you deal with that?

Michael: It's hard because our friends are like, "oh, you scared," and you're trying to show them that you're not, that you can do it. But I've been there before and knew I wasn't supposed to; I knew it was wrong and I felt really bad. **Peer pressure/Moral awareness**

Facilitator: Well, what do you do when you're in that situation? Where someone tried to convince you to smoke, or try alcohol or drugs and you know that's not what you want to do.

Bonnie: I just tell them, No, because I don't want my life to end up that way. **Avoidance strategy/Motivation**

Facilitator: Do you just tell them "No?"

Bonnie: Yeah, I'd be real firm. I'd tell them that I don't want to be that way.

Facilitator: What do some of the rest of you say?

<Probe for other experiences.>

Sasha: I would tell them that I don't want to do it. I would feel like, uneasy. I just try to get out of it the best way I can. But it's very hard, you know, to... because you think these people are your friends, and like...it's hard. **Avoidance/Peer pressure**

Facilitator: So how do you decide? How do you decide what to do?

Sasha: Just stay away from them for a while. **Avoidance**

Facilitator: Sometimes you avoid them.... Anybody else have a different way?

Ian: Get them in trouble. Tell somebody... an adult.

<Nervous, looks at ceiling.>

Facilitator: So you tell an adult so that they can deal with the situation?

<Vague and fidgeting; clearly uncomfortable; possibly unrealistic response; usually would probe for clarity and details.>

Ian: I'd tell an adult—the first one I saw cuz that's what you are supposed to do. My teacher said never let a friend stay in trouble.

Responsibility/Moral awareness

Michael: "Who would you tell? Where would you find somebody?"

Ian: I'd find somebody all right and I'd tell.

<Voice raised.>

Facilitator: Ian, that's a great idea… to help a friend. Do you know of anyone who did something like that?

<Facilitator affirms child's statement to comfort child—not usual in focus group session. Facilitator chooses to ask third-person question, not direct experience because it will be less threatening.>

Ian: No—not yet. But I would.

Facilitator: Are you almost ready to tell me about your pictures?

<Children start describing drawings.>

Jose: Football player for the Steelers with lots of money.   **Fame/money**

Brad: Rich basketball player.   **Fame/money**

Bonnie: Own my own shop, Gel, Hair, and Weave. Horses make our products.

<Much laughter.>

Sasha: Entertainer.   **Fame**

Ian: Rich businessman.   **Money**

Jose: Drive race cars.   **Fame**

Facilitator: I asked you what you thought you wanted your life to be like when you got older. What do you have to do in order to really reach that goal or make that dream come true?

Ian: Get a degree. **Education**

Facilitator: So you need to go to college. **Education**

Ian: You gotta learn all this stuff, then you can be whatever you want. **Education**

Jose: You have to know what you want to be so you can achieve. **Focus**

Bonnie: You have to stay focused. Stay focused on what you want to do. **Focus**

Facilitator: What do you think you need—and I'm not talking money and a fabulous house—to achieve what you really want for your life?

Jose: A degree in something. **Education**

Michael: What he said, a degree, and your family helping you. **Education/Family support**

Bonnie: I think what he said, and I think your mom, your dad, your role models. **Family support**

<Children beginning to get restless.>

<Facilitator thanks group and indicates that she is turning tape off.>

Figure 6.1   Sample audit trail

Text	Codes	Category
Friends smoking/stealing/doing drugs Friends want you to do bad things	Family/friends/ neighborhood pressure	Challenges
Gotta get them out Knew I wasn't supposed to	Responsibility and moral awareness	Strengths
Run away, stay away from trouble Say no/be firm Tell an adult	Strategies—avoid trouble	Strengths
Do your homework/Get a degree/ Education Know what you want/Stay focused	Strategies—to succeed	Strengths
Don't want to be that way Want money/fame/own business Can be what you want	Motivation to succeed/ possibilities	Strengths
Help with homework Family/teacher helping you	Resources available	Strengths

Audit Trail

The audit trail for this example (Box 6.2) would include the verbatim transcript, facilitator's notes, codes, relationship of codes to categories, and tentative themes.

Box 6.2

Notes on session: The group was cooperative, friendly, and seemed to enjoy the session. The facilitator easily established rapport with the children. Usually the children spoke freely with a few exceptions, when the children did not want to share more, because they were clearly uncomfortable and possibly embarrassed by some of their actions. One comment often led to another comment about problems. There was enough detail and vivid description to feel comfortable that there was not a "bandwagon" effect of merely adding on and exaggerating problems.

There is some evidence of the sense of responsibility to help friends and others in trouble, as well as expectations or hope that family would help and support their children. Responsibility and hope might be strengths found in one's community. These concepts will need to be further explored.

The possibility of being able to achieve anything if one can stay on track, and the ambitious dreams, may be unrealistic given the poverty level and challenges in the community. The children appeared hopeful and optimistic, although not well grounded in the process of achieving their dreams. There is an awareness of the importance of education, the need to stay focused and out of trouble, and what trouble means.

Code definitions: These are very straightforward at this stage. Definitions will be refined as the analysis progresses.

Relationship of codes to categories: The codes are easily grouped into the categories, although so far it is clear that more information is needed on each of the six categories, because the categories are not fully developed. Further data collection would target (1) how children perceive and plan to meet challenges to avoid trouble and how they can achieve their dreams; and (2) how the local agency could build strengths and identify an optimal match of resources and needs.

> *Tentative themes*: A theme has very tentatively emerged: meeting challenges to succeed. It does not seem well grounded, and more data are needed to explore how this theme might play out in the lives of these children.

Summary

The challenge in analysis is the development of useful findings from a complex setting. Having only few guidelines available requires the researcher to thoroughly understand the psychosocial context; the various analytic methods available; and the importance of methodological coherence of purpose, process, and product. Keep mind that the purpose is to understand the participants' experiences and to communicate the findings so that they may be readily used. The next chapter addresses several aspects of presenting findings so that they may be best utilized.

7. Communication of Research Findings

This chapter provides guidance on communicating the findings of focus group research to enhance the usefulness of the research. The emphasis is on issues unique to focus groups, parameters of credibility, and suggestions for maximizing usefulness of the findings.

Key Questions

7.1. How do you use the study purpose and knowledge of your intended audience to help structure your writing?

7.2. How and why do you select quotes to be included?

General Comments

We have found a number of good sources that discuss academic writing in general (for example, Silvia, 2007) and writing or communicating the results of qualitative studies (for instance, Holliday, 2007; Miles and Huberman, 1994; Wolcott, 2009). There is little, however, that focuses specifically on presenting the results of focus group research. In this chapter, we highlight insights from available sources that have particular relevance for the communication of focus group results. Throughout we discuss factors that can enhance the credibility of the focus group research report.

Depending on the purpose and the primary audience, the research communication may be written, oral, or electronic. Here, we devote our attention to written communication, assuming that such a report would likely serve as the foundation for other communications. Krueger and Casey (2009) note that written reports can take a variety of forms: narrative, top-line, bulleted, or report letter. Our discussion focuses on the narrative report. Other forms of reporting (written or otherwise) could easily be adapted or excerpted from the narrative report. We do acknowledge, however, that in some instances there is not time to produce a thorough, comprehensive narrative report.

Planning for reporting needs to occur before the actual writing begins; that is, you need to have some sense of the ideal structure of the report in mind, because this may have bearing on the questions asked and the nature of follow-ups to the member's comments. To begin, we encourage you to revisit the original purpose of the project for help in shaping the form and content of the research report. Wolcott (2009) suggests that if you cannot state the purpose of the research in a sentence ("The purpose of this study is . . ."), then further conceptualization may be necessary. This point is reinforced by Thorne (2008). If the purpose of the research project was primarily descriptive, themes and general concepts will dominate the report. In these instances, the primary goal is to represent the range of the member's insights and contributions. If the purpose of the project was theory development, the report will certainly include themes and concepts and will go on to provide more intricate details of the underlying theory and how the concepts and themes provide evidence for the proposed theory.

As with other qualitative methods, the writing of the report tends to be an iterative process (Holliday, 2007; see Figure 5.1, p. 90). You will sort and organize the data (using various manual or electronic tools) and write based on initial impressions. Miles and Huberman (1994) will likely be helpful in this effort. As you continue to work with the data, you will likely have occasion to reflect and then reorganize as new insights emerge. We encourage you to allow plenty of time in your project timeline for writing and rewriting. This advice is, of course, not unique to focus groups or even to qualitative methods. However, it is particularly important in reporting focus group research, because it will generally take more than one round to adequately capture an understanding of what the members said and synthesize it all into a concise yet comprehensive and useful report.

As with other qualitative methods, the data gathered in focus group is obviously text, which can sometimes be overwhelming to summarize and synthesize. Wolcott (2009) evokes advice given to novice travelers in relation to this issue: when in doubt, leave it out. Wolcott suggests that is best to look for instances or cases that can represent the whole, so that you can do less more thoroughly.

Rigor

Wolcott (2009) suggests avoiding the tendency to draw sweeping conclusions, which we certainly believe applies to focus groups. In general, focus groups are not designed to come to consensus or some form of agreement, but are for knowledge development. Thus, we support Wolcott's advice to steer away from offering a "grand flourish" at the end, which may tempt you to go beyond the boundaries of the material presented into the area of what should or could be. This temptation can be particularly strong if the findings are positive or as expected (Wolcott, 2009). Wolcott encourages working toward a conservative closing statement that succinctly reviews the findings.

Ethics

Remember to preserve anonymity of the group members, to the extent possible and as requested by the members. As we have noted in earlier chapters, not all aspects of this necessity are within the researcher's control, as Tolich (2009) has outlined. In relation to reporting, it is particularly important not to include detailed descriptive information that could reveal the identity of a member or tie a member to a specific comment. In some instances, to protect the members, pseudonyms might be used or details adapted (without changing the meaning).

Researchers have an obligation to the focus group members to carry out high-quality research and to accurately and appropriately represent their experiences. This requirement can be a challenge in the case of unanticipated or unflattering findings, particularly if a specific group who hoped for a different outcome commissioned the study. This information must be conveyed, albeit perhaps carefully, in a manner that appropriately represents the members' perspectives.

Immediately following is an outline of the necessary sections in a typical research report, a structure that is fairly consistent across methodological approaches. Contents within the designated sections that are unique to focus group reports are highlighted.

Outline of Narrative Report

Title Page

The best advice we can offer here is to follow the guidelines of your professional organization, the journal you are submitting your work to, the conference submission guidelines your course instructor, or the preferences of the group that commissioned the focus groups. In general, however, a title page includes the title of the report, the purpose of the report (academic paper, or who commissioned the research), author(s), and date.

Executive Summary (or Abstract)

Typically best when written last, the abstract (or executive summary) is a short summary that hits the key points of the entire report. Although it appears right after the title page, it is best written last, because once the report is finished it is easier to extract the key ideas and have the summary directly parallel the full report.

Table of Contents

This is self-explanatory and may not be necessary for short reports. Many word processing programs can produce this for you, with proper formatting codes, thus obviating the problem of editing the table of contents each time you change something in the body of the report.

Purpose and Methodology

Depending on complexity (and the dictates of your intended audience) the Purpose might be a separate section. Regardless, it should clearly detail the initial reason for and focus of the research. Whether a separate section or combined, the Methodology section should flow logically and directly from the Purpose; that is, it should be clear to the reader why focus groups were chosen as the methodological approach. Finally, an overview of the research procedures and process should also be included. The goal here, as with all research reports, is to provide enough detail that the reader can replicate your study.

Research Findings

This section should review in some detail the research findings. The findings will need to, in some form, speak directly to the initial research focus and the guideline questions. In some instances, at least for the initial draft, you may want to organize your data and your writing by the guideline questions.

The total number of focus groups conducted, the range of number of persons in each session, and some basic demographic information about the participants should be reported. In addition, the recruitment strategy and its success will help the reader to understand the sampling process. In describing the participants, any demographic information pertinent to the project focus should be reported in aggregate form. Beyond the variables discussed in this paragraph, focus group research findings should not be communicated in quantitative form.

As already noted, the report should include the guideline questions asked. The questions should be included both in their original form along with any revisions that evolved later in the project. A description of what insight or events led to the revision should also be included.

Use quotations judiciously, so that they highlight the "story" you are telling, but they should not actually drive the story. Without having to deal with unnecessary detail, the reader/recipient should be able to follow the reasoning that led to a particular conclusion or interpretation. Transparency is definitely key (White, Woodfield, and Ritchie, 2003). In some instances, it is necessary to include an exchange between participants, not just isolated quotations, thus highlighting both the synergy between or among group members and one of the ultimate reasons for using focus group in this instance—as opposed to another research approach.

Recommendations for Future Research

This section might also be labeled "Discussion" depending on the formatting requirements of your intended audience. Here you should address what wisdom can be gleaned from the research you conducted, the implications of your research in relation to the broader body of knowledge on this topic, and what questions need to be address in future studies. Any weakness in your study that might be corrected or addressed in future studies could also be discussed here. This section might also highlight any questions raised or left unanswered by your study.

Appendix

This section may be optional, depending on the format and length of any accompanying documents. It is generally easier for readers if the pertinent materials can be included in the body of the text, if feasible. If it is not feasible, sometimes a brief excerpt from this accompanying document with a notation of where the full documentation is located will simplify things for the reader.

8. Concluding Thoughts

One of our goals in this book is to provide information about how to appropriately use focus groups as a research tool. We hope that by defining what *is* the proper use of focus groups we have also defined what *is not*. Both of us have encountered examples of data-collection strategies that are called "focus groups" but that do not meet the spirit or the letter of what we have outlined here. We realize that the method seems deceptively simple, which undoubtedly contributes to its misuse on occasion. Our hope is that we have described the structure necessary to use the technique effectively while also providing enough detail to allow you to be flexible as the situation warrants.

A second goal is to communicate the value of focus groups as a research approach. We both come to this work from rather traditional backgrounds in quantitative methodologies, and we respect those approaches when they are used properly. Nonetheless, we have come to understand the value of qualitative approaches in general and focus groups in particular, in relation to certain research questions. By now it should be clear that we believe focus groups to be a technique that yields rich data that could not be obtained through other means.

That being said, we do not believe this book to be the end of the discussion needed on focus groups. Although it is well documented that focus groups can be a very useful tool for research in many settings, most of the literature on guidelines and recommendations—including much of this book—is based on experience rather than empirical research that provides a rational for the guidelines. Although many of the recommendations in this book are informed by a psychosocial context, more research is needed to move the method forward (Heary and Hennessy, 2002).

Future research should focus on the impact of various data-elicitation stimulus techniques (drawing a picture, watching a movie, and so on) in relation to the common practice of using only guideline questions. Research is also needed on the effects of different group sizes, composition of session participants (homogenous versus mixed groups in terms of roles and socioeconomic status), previous familiarity among members, and multiple sessions for a group. The outcomes to be explored could include the evaluation of the quality and comprehensiveness of information in relation to the study purpose. Findings could compare results across the dimensions mentioned above and also be compared with information collected with interviews. However, comparison with quantitative approaches (for example, questionnaire) would not be appropriate, because study purposes would differ.

We began this book by comparing the hidden codes in some quilts created during the era of slavery in the United States with the ability to ferret out deeper meanings in social science research by using focus groups. We hope that this book has provided the background and insight to guide your future efforts in finding the hidden meanings. May you have gained as much by reading this book as we have by writing it.

Glossary

category Collection of data that has been grouped based on similarity; further examination helps to determine the major commonalities in the data.

codes Meanings assigned to each unit of data.

conforming Stating agreement with the comments expressed in the group, even though the speaker does not truly believe the statement; also, a process of cognitive restructuring when a member's opinion is influenced by other members.

content analysis Systematic classification of codes and themes, using subjective interpretation.

discourse analysis Analysis of the function of language and how conversation is constructed.

focus group Data collection technique using a group session with a facilitator and a selected topic.

grounded theory Various inductive, systematic approaches to develop concepts and theory.

group dynamics Processes within a group involving acting and reacting influenced by norms, roles, relations, development, need to belong, and social influence.

inductive analysis Process that begins with data and explores relationships to form categories and models.

internal confidentiality A concern for the possibility of disclosing more than intended.

mixed methods Planned use of multiple approaches to data collection and analysis.

narrative analysis Analysis that focuses on the meaning of the story, with a plot and a time sequence.

probing Following up on guideline questions to clarify or further explore the comments.

reflectivity Self-scrutiny to become aware of one's own beliefs and biases.

rigor Use of verification strategies to enhance the validity of the research process and findings.

sampling In qualitative research, the intentional collection of data to explore the topic of interest.

self-censoring Process that occurs when a group member is influenced by the perception of what the group expects from him or her and thus chooses not to share a conflicting or embarrassing experience.

special populations Persons whose welfare requires special considerations.

symbolic interaction Dynamic process involved in making meaning that is embedded in the culture and each person's experiences.

synergy Enhancement activity due to the group interaction.

thematic analysis Umbrella term referring to identifying broad constructs.

theme Broad construct that cuts across codes and categories.

vulnerable populations *See* special populations.

References

Albarracin, D., Durantini, M. R., Earl, A., and Gunnoe, J. B. (2008). Beyond the most willing audiences: A meta-intervention to increase exposure to HIV-prevention programs by vulnerable populations. *Health Psychology, 27*(5), 638–644.

Allen, L. (2006). Trying not to think "straight": Conducting focus groups with lesbian and gay youth. *International Journal of Qualitative Studies in Education, 19*(2), 163–176.

Andreas, D. C., Abraham, N. S., Naik, A. D., Street, R. L., and Sharf, B. F. (2010). Understanding risk communication through patient narratives about complex antithrombotic therapies. *Qualitative Health Research, 20*(8), 1156–1165.

Asbury, J., and Carey, M. A. (2005, October). *Using focus groups with children: Insights and Cautionary tales.* Paper presented at joint meeting of American Evaluation Association and the Canadian Evaluation Society, Toronto, Canada.

Asch, S. E. (1951). Effects of group pressure upon the modification and distortion of judgments. In H. Guetzkow (Ed.), *Groups, leadership and men.* Pittsburgh: Carnegie Press.

Ayling, R., and Mewse, A. J. (2009). Evaluating Internet interviews with gay men. *Qualitative Health Research, 19*(4), 566–576.

Baldry, E., Green, S., and Thorpe, K. (2006). Urban Australian Aboriginal peoples' experience of human services. *International Journal of Social Work, 49*(3), 364–375.

Barel, E., Van Ijzendoorn, M. H., Sagi-Schwartz, A., and Bakermans-Kraneburg, M. J. (2010). Surviving the holocaust: A meta-analysis of the long-term sequelae of a genocide. *Psychological Bulletin, 136*(5), 677–698.

Bito, S., Matsumura, S., Singer, M. K., Meredith, L. S., Fukuhara, S., and Wenger, N. S. (2007). Acculturation and end-of-life decision making: Comparison of Japanese and Japanese-American focus groups. *Bioethics, 21*(5), 251–262.

Blumer, H. (1969). *Symbolic interaction.* Berkeley and Los Angeles: University of California Press.

Bogdan, R. C., and Biklen, S. K. (2007). *Qualitative research for education: An introduction to theories and methods,* 5th ed. Boston: Allyn and Bacon.

Braun, V., and Clarke, V. (2006). Using thematic analysis in psychology. *Qualitative Research in Psychology, 3,* 77–101.

Brondani, M. A., MacEntee, M. I., Brynant, S. R., and O'Neill, B. (2008). Using written vignettes in focus groups among older adults to discuss oral health as a sensitive topic. *Qualitative Health Research, 18,* 1145–1153.

Bruner, J. S. (1990). *Acts of meaning.* Cambridge, MA: Harvard University Press.

Bullock, K., McGraw, S. A., Blank, K., and Bradley, E. H. (2005). What matters to older African Americans facing end-of-life decisions? A focus groups study. *Journal of Social Work in End-of-Life and Palliative Care, 1*(3), 3–19.

Carey, M. A. (1990, August). *Cognitive aspects of questionnaire design: Surveying the elderly.* Paper presented at the American Psychological Conference, Boston, MA.

———. (1994). The group effect in focus groups: Planning, implementing, and interpreting focus group research. In J. Morse (Ed.), *Critical issues in qualitative research.* Thousand Oaks, CA: Sage Publications.

———. (1995). Comments in the analysis of focus group data. *Qualitative Health Research, 5*(4), 487–495.

Carey, M. A., and Langert-DeGori (2000). Using focus groups to improve patient services. 6th Annual Qualitative Health Research Conference, Banff, Canada.

Carey, M. A., and Smith, M. W. (1992). Enhancement of validity through qualitative approaches: Incorporating the patient's perspective. *Evaluation and the Health Professions, 15,* 107–114.

———. (1994). Capturing the group effect in focus groups: A special concern in analysis. *Qualitative Health Research, 4*(1), 123–127.

Carey, M. A., and Swanson, J. M. (2003). Funding qualitative research. *Qualitative Health Research, 13*(6), 852–857.

Castellblanch, R., and Abrahamson, D. J. (2003). What focus groups suggest about mental health parity policymaking. *Professional Psychology: Research and Practice, 34*(5), 540–547.

Charmaz, K. (2006). *Constructing grounded theory: A practical guide through qualitative analysis.* Thousand Oaks, CA: Sage Publications.

Clark, C. (1972). Black Studies or the study of Black people? In R. L. Jones (Ed.), *Black Psychology* (pp. 3–17). New York: Harper & Row.

Corbin, J., and Morse, J. (2003). The unstructured interactive interview: Issues of reciprocity and risks when dealing with sensitive topics. *Qualitative Inquiry, 9,* 335–354.

Corbin, J., and Strauss, A. (2008). *Basics of qualitative research,* 3rd ed. Thousand Oaks, CA: Sage Publications.

Creswell, J. W. (2008). *Research design: Qualitative, quantitative, and mixed methods approaches,* 3rd ed. Thousand Oaks, CA: Sage Publications.

Cretchley, J., Gallois, C., Chenery, H., and Smith, A. (2010). Conversations between carers and people with schizophrenia: A qualitative analysis using Leximancer. *Qualitative Health Research, 20*(2), 1611–1628.

REFERENCES

Darbyshire, P., MacDougall, C., and Schiller, W. (2005). Multiple methods in qualitative research with children: More insights or just more? *Qualitative Research,* 5(4), 417–436.

Datta, L. (1994). Paradigm wars: A basis for peaceful coexistence and beyond. *New Directions for Program Evaluation, 61,* 53–70.

Deitrick, L. M., Paxton, H. D., Rivera, A., Gertner, E. J., Biery, N., Letcher, A. S., and Salas-Lopez, D. (2010). Understanding the role of *Promotora* in a Latino Diabetes education program. *Qualitative Health Research, 20*(3), 123–127.

Driessnack, M. (2006). Draw-and-tell conversations with children about fear. *Qualitative Health Research, 16*(10), 1414–1435.

Duggleby, W. (2005). What about focus group interaction data? *Qualitative Health Research, 15* (6), 832–840.

Dunlap, E., Johnson, B. D., Kotarba, J. A., and Fackler, J. (2009). Making connections: New Orleans evacuees' experiences in obtaining drugs. *Journal of Psychoactive Drugs, 41* (3), 219–226.

Edwards, R. (1998). A critical examination of the use of interpreters in the qualitative research process. *Journal of Ethnic and Migration Studies, 24*(1), 197–208.

Elo, S., and Kyngas, H. (2007). The qualitative content analysis process. *Journal of Advanced Nursing, 62,* 107–115.

Fairclough, N. (1993). *Discourse and social change.* Cambridge: Polity.

Farnsworth, J., and Boon, B. (2010). Analysing group dynamics in the focus groups. *Qualitative Research, 10*(5), 605–624.

Fenton, A., Arnold, P., Fairbank, S., and Shaw, T. (2009). Using focus groups and photography to evaluate experiences of social inclusion within rehabilitation adult mental health services. *Mental Health Review Journal, 14*(3), 13–22.

Festinger, L. (1957). *A theory of cognitive dissonance.* Evanston, IL: Row Peterson.

Fitzpatrick, E., Olds, J., Durieux-Smith, A., McCrae, R., Schramm, D., and Gaboury, I. (2009). Pediatric cochlear implantation: How much hearing is too much? *International Journal of Audiology, 48,* 91–97.

Fox, F. E., Morris, M., and Rumsey, N. (2007). Doing synchronous focus groups with young people: Methodological reflections. *Qualitative Health Research, 17*(4), 539–547.

Franklin, K. K., and Lowry, C. (2001). Computer-mediated focus group sessions: Naturalistic inquiry in a networked environment. *Qualitative Research, 1*(2), 169–184.

Frazier, L. M., Miller, V. A., Horbelt, D. V., Delmore, J. E., Miller, B. E., and Paschal, A. M. (2010). Comparison of focus groups on cancer and employment conducted face to face or by telephone. *Qualitative Health Research, 20*(5), 617–627.

Gany, F. M., Herrera, A. P., Avallone, M., and Changrani, J. (2006). Attitudes, knowledge, and health-seeking behavior of five immigrant communities in the prevention and screening of cancer: A focus group approach. *Ethnicity and Health, 11*(1), 19–39.

Gibbs, S. M., Brown, M. J., and Muir, W. J. (2008). The experiences of adults with intellectual disabilities and their careers in general hospitals: A focus group study. *Journal of Intellectual Disability Research, 52*(12), 1061–1077.

Glaser, B. G. (1995). *Grounded theory: 1984–1994.* Mill Valley Press, CA: Sociology Press.

Guba, E. G., and Lincoln, Y. S. (1989). *Fourth generation evaluation.* Newbury Park, CA: Sage Publications.

Guise, J., McKinlay, A., and Widdicombe, S. (2010). The impact of early stroke on identity: A discourse analytic study. *Health, 14*(1), 75–90.

Halkier, B. (2010). Focus groups as social enactments: Integrating interaction and content in the analysis of focus group data. *Qualitative Research, 10*(1), 71–89.

Hall, W. A., and Callery, P. (2001). Enhancing the rigor of Grounded Theory: Incorporating reflexivity and relationality. *Qualitative Health Research, 11*(2), 257–272.

Hammersley, M. (2010). Reproducing or constructing? Some questions about transcription in social research. *Qualitative Research, 10*(5), 553–569.

Hammersley, M., and Atkinson, P. (1995). *Ethnography: Principles in practice,* 2nd ed. London: Routledge.

Hastie, R. (1986). Experimental evidence on group accuracy. In B. Grossman and G. Owen (Eds.), *Information pooling and group decision making* (pp. 129–264). Greenwich, CT: JAI.

Hawkins, J. D., Catalano, R. F., and Miller, J. Y. (1992). Risk and protective factors for alcohol and other drug problems in adolescence and early adulthood: Implications for practice. *Psychological Bulletin, 112*(1), 64–105.

Heary, C. M., and Hennessy, E. (2002). The use of focus group interviews in pediatric health care research. *Journal of Pediatric Psychology, 27*(1), 47–57.

Hennink, M. M. (2008). Emergent issues in international focus group discussions. In S. N. Hesse-Biber and P. Leavy (Eds.), *Handbook of emergent methods* (pp. 207–220). New York: Gilford.

Hermanowicz, J. C. (2002). The great interview: 25 strategies for studying people in bed. *Qualitative Sociology, 25*(4), 479–499.

Hill, M. (2006). Children's voices on ways of having a voice: Children and young people's perspectives on methods used in research and consultation. *Childhood, 13*(1), 69–89.

Hollander, J. A. (2004). The social context of focus groups. *Journal of Contemporary Ethnography, 33*(5), 602–637.

Holliday, A. (2007). *Doing and writing qualitative research,* 2nd ed. Thousand Oaks, CA: Sage Publications.

Holtgraves, T. (1986). Language structure in social interaction: Perceptions of direct and indirect speech acts and interactants who use them. *Journal of Personality and Social Psychology, 51*(2), 305–314.

REFERENCES

Hoppe, M. J., Wells, E. A., Morrison, D. M., Gillmore, M. R., and Wilsdon, A. (1995). Using focus groups to discuss sensitive topics with children. *Evaluation Review, 19*(1), 102–114.

Horner, S. D. (2000). Using focus group methods with middle school children. *Research in Nursing & Health, 23*, 510–517.

Horstman, M., Aldiss, S., Richardson, A., and Gibson, F. (2008). Methodological issues when using draw and write technique with children aged 6 to 12 years. *Qualitative Health Research, 15*(9), 1277–1288.

Hsieh, H.-F., and Shannon, S. E. (2005). Three approaches to qualitative content analysis. *Qualitative Health Research, 15*(9), 1277–1288.

Hughes, D., and DuMont, K. (1993). Using focus group to facilitate culturally anchored research. *American Journal of Community Psychology, 21*(6), 775–806.

Ivanoff, S. D. (2002). Focus group discussions as a tool for developing a health education programme for elderly persons with visual impairment. *Scandinavian Journal of Occupational Therapy, 9*, 3–9.

James, N., and Bushner, H. (2009). *Online interviewing.* London: Sage Publications.

Janis, L. (1972). *Victims of groupthink: A psychological study of foreign-policy decisions and fiascoes.* Boston: Houghton Mifflin.

Karnielli-Miller, O., Strier, R., and Pessach, L. (2009). Power relations in qualitative research. *Qualitative Health Research, 19*(2), 279–289.

Keim, K. S., Swanson, M. A., Cann, S. E., and Salinas, A. (1999). Focus group methodology: Adapting the process for low-income adults and children of Hispanic and Caucasian ethnicity. *Family and Consumer Sciences Research Journal, 27*(4), 451–465.

Kennedy, C., Kools, S., and Kruger, R. (2001). Methodological considerations in children's focus groups. *Nursing Research, 50*(3), 184–187.

Kidd, P. S., and Parshall, M. B. (2000). Getting the focus and the group: Enhancing analytical rigor in focus group research. *Qualitative Health Research, 10*(3), 293–308.

Kissil, K., Nino, A., Jacobs, S., Davey, M., and Tubbs, C. Y. (2010). "It has been a good growing experience for me": Growth experiences among African American youth coping with parental cancer. *Families, Systems, & Health, 28*(3), 274–289.

Kitzinger, J. (1994). The methodology of focus groups: The importance of interaction between research participants. *Sociology of Health and Illness, 16*(1), 103–121.

Krueger, R. A., and Casey, M. A. (2009). *Focus groups: A practical guide for applied research*, 4th ed. Thousand Oaks, CA: Sage Publications.

Kumpfer, K. L., and Alvarado, R. (2003). Family-strengthening approaches for the prevention of youth problem behaviors. *American Psychologist, 58*(6), 457–465.

Kvale, S. (1995). The social construction of validity. *Qualitative Inquiry, 1*(1), 19–40.

———. (1996). *InterViews: An introduction to qualitative research interviewing.* Thousand Oaks, CA: Sage Publications.

Kvale, S. (2006). Dominance through interviews and dialogues. *Qualitative Inquiry,* *12*(3), 480–500.

Kvale, S., and Brinkmann, S. (2009). *InterViews: Learning the craft of qualitative research interviewing,* 2nd ed. Thousand Oaks, CA: Sage Publications.

Larkin, P., and de Casterle, B. D. (2007). Multilingual translation issues in qualitative research: Reflections on a metaphorical process. *Qualitative Health Research, 4*(1), 123–127.

Leung, K., Wu, E., Lue, B., and Tang, L. (2004). The use of focus groups in evaluating quality of life components among elderly Chinese people. *Quality of Life Research, 13,* 179–190.

Lofland, J., and Lofland, L. H. (1995). *Analyzing social settings: A guide to qualitative observation and analysis, part 2.* Belmont, CA: Wadsworth.

Maxwell, J. A. (2010). Using numbers in qualitative research. *Qualitative Inquiry,* *16*(6), 475–482.

Mayan, M. J. (2009). *Essentials of qualitative inquiry.* Walnut Creek, CA: Left Coast Press.

Mead, G. (1934). *Mind, self, and society.* Chicago: University of Chicago Press.

Merton, R., Fiske, M., and Kendall, P. (1990). *The focused interview: A manual of problems and procedures,* 2nd ed. New York: Free Press.

Miles, M. B., and Huberman, A. M. (1994). *Qualitative data analysis: An expanded sourcebook,* 2nd ed. Thousand Oaks, CA: Sage Publications.

Morgan, D., Fellows, C., and Guevara, H. (2008). Emergent approaches to focus group research. In S. Nagy Hesse-Biber and P. Levy, *Handbook of emergent methods* (pp. 189–206). New York: The Guilford Press.

Morgan, D. L. (1993). *The focus group guidebook.* Thousand Oaks, CA: Sage Publications.

———. (2010). Reconsidering the role of interaction in analyzing and reporting focus groups. *Qualitative Health Research, 20*(5), 718–722.

Morgan, M., Gibbs, S., Maxwell, K., and Britten, N. (2002). Hearing children's voices: Methodological issues in conducting focus groups with children aged 7–11 years. *Qualitative Research, 2*(1), 5–20.

Morin, D., Cobigo, V., Rivard, M., and Lepine, M. (2010). Intellectual disabilities and depression: How to adapt psychological assessment and intervention. *Canadian Psychology, 51*(3), 185–193.

Morrison-Beedy, D., Cote-Arsenault, D., and Feinstein, N. (2001). Maximizing results with focus groups: Moderator and analysis issues. *Applied Nursing Research, 14*(1), 48–53.

Morse, J. (2008). Confusing categories and themes. *Qualitative Health Research, 18*(6), 727–728.

Morse, J., Barrett, M., Mayan, M., Olson, K., and Spiers, J. (2002). Verification strategies for establishing reliability in qualitative research. *International Journal of Qualitative Methodology, 1*(2). Article 2. Accessed January 2006, *www.ualberta.edu.ca/~ijqm.*

REFERENCES

Morse, J. M., and Field, P. A. (1995). *Qualitative research methods for health professionals*, 2nd ed. Thousand Oaks, CA: Sage Publications.

Morse, J. M., and Niehaus, L. (2009). *Mixed method design: Principles and procedures*. Walnut Creek, CA: Left Coast Press.

Nabors, L. A., Ramos, V., and Weist, M. D. (2001). Use of focus groups as a tool for evaluating programs for children and families. *Journal of Educational and Psychological Consultation, 12*(3), 243–256.

Nelson-Gardell, D. (2001). The voices of victims: Surviving child sexual abuse. *Child and Adolescent Social Work Journal, 18*(6), 401–416.

Odell, A. P. (2008). *The contemporary perspective of wellness through the voices of the Kupuna*. Unpublished dissertation. University of San Diego, San Diego, CA.

Ong, A. D., Fuller-Rowell, T., and Burrow, A. L. (2009). Racial discrimination and the stress process. *Journal of Personality and Social Psychology, 96*(6), 1259–1271.

Orel, N. A. (2004). Gay, lesbian and bisexual elders: Expressed needs and concerns across focus groups. *Journal of Gerontological Social Work, 43*(2/3), 57–77.

Patton, M. Q. (2002). *Qualitative research & evaluation methods*, 3rd ed. Thousand Oaks, CA: Sage Publications.

Pfefferbaum, B., Houston, J. B., Wyche, K. F., Van Horn, R. L., Reyes, G., Jeon-Slaughter, H., and North, C. S. (2008). Children displaced by Hurricane Katrina: A focus group study. *Journal of Loss and Trauma, 13*, 303–308.

Poland, B. (1995). Transcription quality as an aspect of rigor in qualitative research. *Qualitative Inquiry, 1*(3), 290–310.

Reissman, C. (1993). *Narrative analysis*. Newbury Park, CA: Sage Publications.

Rubin, H. J., and Rubin, I. S. (2005). *Qualitative interviewing: The art of hearing data*, 2nd ed. Thousand Oaks, CA: Sage Publications.

Schneider, S. J., Kerwin, J., Frechtling, J., and Vivari, B. A. (2002). Characteristics of the discussion in online and face-to-face focus groups. *Social Science Computer Review, 20*(1), 31–42.

Shklarov, S. (2007). Double vision uncertainty: The bilingual researcher and the ethics of cross-language research. *Qualitative Health Research, 17*(4), 529–538.

Shrank, W. H., Kutner, J. S., Richardson, T., Mularski, R. A., Fischer, S., and Kagawa-Singer, M. (2005). Focus group findings about the influence of culture on communication preferences in end-of-life care. *Journal of Internal Medicine, 20*, 703–709.

Silvia, P. J. (2007). *How to write a lot*. Washington, D.C.: American Psychological Association.

Smith, M. W. (1995). Ethics in focus groups: A few concerns. *Qualitative Health Research, 5*(4), 478–486.

Spradley, J. P. (1979). *The ethnographic interview*. New York: Holt, Rinehart, & Winston.

Stacciarini, J. R. (2008). Focus groups: Examining a community-based group intervention for depressed Puerto Rican woman. *Issues in Mental Health Nursing, 29,* 679–700.

Starks, H., and Trinidad, S. B. (2010). Choose your method: A comparison of phenomenology, discourse analysis, and Grounded Theory. *Qualitative Health Research, 17*(10), 1372–1380.

Stewart, D. W., Shamdasani, P. N., and Rook, D. W. (2007). *Focus groups: Theory and practice,* 2nd ed. Thousand Oaks, CA: Sage Publications.

Stewart, K., and Williams, M. (2005). Researching online populations: The use of online focus groups for social research. *Qualitative Research, 5*(4), 395–416.

Strickland, C. J., Walsh, E., and Cooper, M. (2006). Healing fractured families: Parents and elders' perspectives on the impact of colonization and youth suicide prevention in a Pacific Northwest American Indian tribe. *Journal of Transcultural Nursing, 17*(1), 5–12.

Sue, S. (1983). Ethnic minority issues in psychology. *American Psychologist, 38*(3), 583–592.

Tesch, R. (1991). (Ed.) Computers and qualitative data. *Qualitative Sociology, 14*(3 and 4) Fall and Winter.

Thorne, S. (2008). *Interpretive description.* Walnut Creek, CA: Left Coast Press.

Tilley, S. A. (2003). "Challenging" research practices: Turning a critical lens on the work of transcription. *Qualitative Inquiry, 9*(5), 750–773.

Tobin, J. L., and Dobard, R. G. (1999). *Hidden in plain view: A secret story of quilts and the underground railroad.* New York: Random House.

Tolich, M. (2009). The principle of caveat emptor: Confidentiality and informed consent as endemic ethical dilemmas in focus group research. *Bioethical Inquiry, 6,* 99–108.

Twinn, S. (2000). The analysis of focus group data: A challenge to the rigour of qualitative research. *Nursing Times Research, 5*(2), 140–146.

Underhill, C., and Olmsted, M. G. (2003). An experimental comparison of computer-mediated and face-to-face focus groups. *Social Science Computer Review, 21*(4), 506–512.

Valaitis, R. K., and Sword, W. A. (2005). Online discussions with pregnant and parenting adolescents: Perspectives and possibilities. *Health Promotion Practice, 6*(4), 464–471.

VandeVen, A. H., and Delbecq, A. L. (1974). The effectiveness of nominal, delphi, and interacting group decision-making processes. *The Academy of Management Journal, 17*(4), 605–621.

Vogt, D. S., King, D. W., and King, L. A. (2004). Focus groups in psychological assessment: Enhancing content validity by consulting members of the target population. *Psychological Assessment, 16*(3), 231–243.

Walston, J. T., and Lissitz, R. W. (2000). Computer-mediated focus groups. *Evaluation Review, 24*(5), 457–483.

REFERENCES

Warr, D. J. (2005). "It was fun . . . but we don't usually talk about these things": Analyzing sociable interaction in focus groups. *Qualitative Inquiry, 11*(2), 200–225.

Wertheimer, M. (1938). *A source book of Gestalt psychology.* Vol. 4. London: Routledge & Kegan Paul.

———. (1923). Laws of organization in perceptual forms. First published as Untersuchungen zur Lehre von der Gestalt II, in Psycologische Forschung, pp. 301–350. Translation published in Ellis, W. (1938).

White, C., Woodfield, K., and Ritchie, J. (2003). Reporting and presenting qualitative data. In J. Ritchie and J. Lewis (Eds.), *Qualitative research practice* (pp. 287–320). Thousand Oaks, CA: Sage Publications.

Wolcott, H. E. (2009). *Writing up qualitative research.* Los Angeles: Sage Publications.

Wong, J. P., and Poon, M. K.-L. (2010). Bringing translation out of the shadows: Translation as an issue of methodological significance in cross-cultural qualitative research. *Qualitative Health Research, 20*(8), 151–158.

Wutich, A., Lant, T., White, D. D., Larson, K. L., and Garting, M. (2010). Comparing focus group and individual responses on sensitive topics: A study of water decision makers in a desert city. *Field Methods, 22*(1), 88–110.

Yuen, F. C. (2004). "It was fun . . . I liked drawing my thoughts": Using drawings as a part of a focus group process with children. *Journal of Leisure Research, 36*(4), 461–482.

Index

About the Authors

Martha Ann Carey's (Ph.D., R.N.) experience developing, implementing, and evaluating social science research was gained from her years of working with public health agencies of the U.S. government, including the National Institute of Mental Health, the National Institute of Nursing Research, the Substance Abuse and Mental Health Services Administration, and the U.S. Government Accountability Office. Her pragmatic approach to research design and her education in qualitative and quantitative research methods were put to use in academia, where she taught research design and qualitative methods courses in doctoral education and nursing programs and served as an investigator for federally funded grants. Her international work includes presentations and qualitative research workshops. Dr. Carey was the first fellow at the International Institute of Qualitative Methodology, in Edmonton, Canada, supported by a U.S. Public Health Services International Fellowship Award in 1998. She continues to work with nonprofit organizations and mentor researchers through her work with Kells Consulting, a services research and training firm in Pennsylvania.

Jo-Ellen Asbury (Ph.D.) currently serves as Assistant Vice President for Academic Affairs and Professor of Psychology at Stevenson University (Stevenson, MD), where she heads the Office of Institutional Research and Assessment. Her current scholarship is focused in the areas of higher education assessment and program evaluation. Before joining Stevenson University, she was a Professor of Psychology at Bethany College, where she also served two terms as Chair of the Psychology Department, two terms as Chair of the Faculty Personnel Committee, and two years as Director for Faculty Assessment. During her time at Bethany, Dr. Asbury's scholarship focused primarily on domestic violence in families of color and focus groups as a methodological approach. In 1997 she was awarded a research fellowship at by the Womanist Studies Program at the University of Georgia, and in 1994 she participated in a faculty exchange program with the University of Canterbury, Christchurch, New Zealand. Dr. Asbury also served on the faculty of the College of Wooster. In addition to her academic positions, Dr. Asbury has worked at the Army Research Institute and the U.S. Government Accountability Office.

In addition to her work at Stevenson University, Dr. Asbury also works as an independent consultant doing program evaluation work with non-profit agencies and with colleges and university on issues of assessment of academic programs.